SEWING EXPRESS

Nancy Zieman

Dedication

In memory of June Tailor, one of the first sewing entrepreneurs, who began producing her line of timesaving pressing, sewing, and quilting notions in 1961. She was a great mentor paving the way so that others could follow.

Sewing Express
©1994 by Oxmoor House, Inc.
Book Division of Southern Progress Corporation
P.O. Box 2463, Birmingham, Alabama 35201

Published by Oxmoor House, Inc., and Leisure Arts, Inc.

Library of Congress Number: 94-68178
Hardcover ISBN: 0-8487-1402-4
Softcover ISBN: 0-8487-1413-X
Manufactured in the United States of America
First Printing 1994

Editor-in-Chief: Nancy J. Fitzpatrick
Senior Crafts Editor: Susan Ramey Wright
Senior Editor, Editorial Services: Olivia Kindig Wells
Art Director: James Boone

Sewing Express

Editor: Linda Baltzell Wright
Editorial Assistant: Rhonda Richards Wamble
Copy Editor: L. Amanda Owens
Copy Assistant: Jennifer K. Mathews
Designer: Emily Albright
Senior Photographer: John O'Hagan
Photostylist: Katie Stoddard
Production and Distribution Director: Phillip Lee
Production Manager: Gail Morris
Associate Production Manager: Theresa L. Beste
Production Assistant: Marianne Jordan

Illustrator: Rochelle Stibb
Editorial Assistance, Nancy's Notions: Susan Roemer
Dressmaking: Donna Fenske
        Phyllis Steinbach
        Nancy Zieman

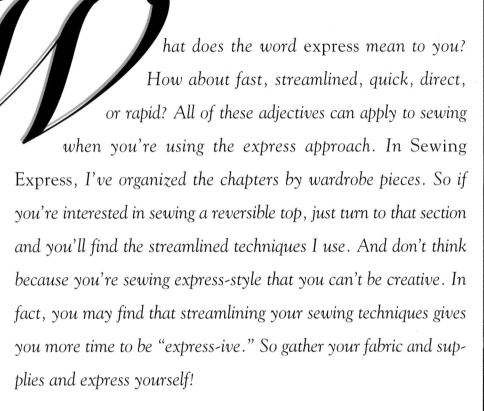

*W*hat does the word express mean to you? How about fast, streamlined, quick, direct, or rapid? All of these adjectives can apply to sewing when you're using the express approach. In Sewing Express, I've organized the chapters by wardrobe pieces. So if you're interested in sewing a reversible top, just turn to that section and you'll find the streamlined techniques I use. And don't think because you're sewing express-style that you can't be creative. In fact, you may find that streamlining your sewing techniques gives you more time to be "express-ive." So gather your fabric and supplies and express yourself!

Happy sewing!

Nancy Zieman

CONTENTS

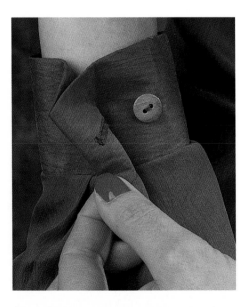

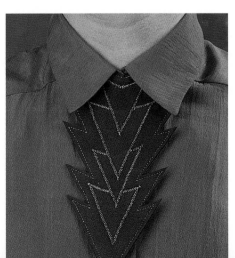

Blouses

Sewing in the fast lane doesn't mean giving up quality, just changing the traditional time-consuming techniques to express-style techniques. Let's begin with classic blouse patterns and you'll soon see that sewing express-style is fast, fun, and creative! Best of all, you'll only have to invest a minimum of time to create a fashion statement!

ront Plackets

Pronto Placket

First, let's look at a classic blouse or dress front placket where the neckline is finished with a collar band or with a collar with an attached band. This functional focal point can be streamlined so that the facing, the interfacing, and the placket area are sewn all in one. A few simple steps will transform the front pattern, which generally has multiple pieces, into a single pattern—all without purchasing additional fabric!

Pronto placket

1. To create a placket extension:

• Cut a work sheet 3⅝" wide and as long as the front pattern piece.

• Tape the extension to the blouse (or the dress) front at the center front.

• Cut both fronts from this new pattern piece (**Diagram A**).

> *Note from Nancy: I cut my placket extension from a length of nonwoven, sew-in interfacing. Rather than permanently taping it to a pattern, I pin it in place. After cutting out the pattern, I pin it to my bulletin board so that it's handy when I need it again.*

2. To mark the right front (buttonhole side) placket, make nips (¼" clips) 1¼", 2½", and 3¾" from the center edge at the neckline and the hemline (**Diagram B**).

3. To press and stitch the right placket:

• Place the fabric wrong side up, fold the blouse along the first set of nips, and press to create the interfacing (**Diagram C**).

• Fold along the second set of nips and press to create the facing.

• Fold along the third set of nips to form the placket; press.

• Topstitch the placket ¼" from the outer fold (**Diagram D**).

• Fold out placket. On the right side, topstitch ¼" along the newly formed outer edge (**Diagram E**).

4. Trim ½" from the left front (button side). This trimming eliminates the amount allowed for the tuck, which is not needed on the button side.

> *Note from Nancy: I highly recommend trimming the ½" from the left front **after** the right front has been stitched. Once I trimmed the ½" during cutting, and I cut the wrong side. That blouse buttoned left to right!*

(Continued on page 10)

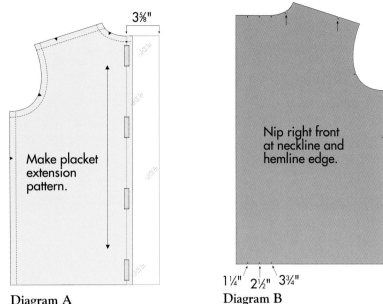

3⅝"

Make placket extension pattern.

Diagram A

Nip right front at neckline and hemline edge.

1¼" 2½" 3¾"

Diagram B

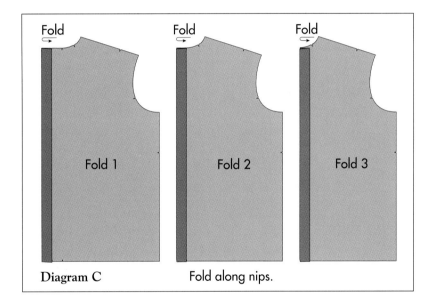

Fold Fold Fold

Fold 1 Fold 2 Fold 3

Diagram C Fold along nips.

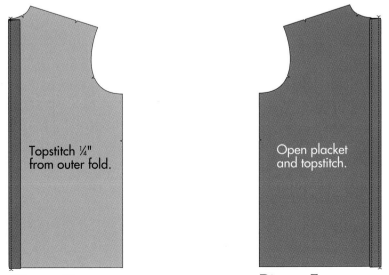

Topstitch ¼" from outer fold.

Diagram D

Open placket and topstitch.

Diagram E

Pronto Placket (*continued*)

5. To mark the left front placket, make nips 1¼" and 2½" from the center cut edge at the neckline and the hemline **(Diagram F)**.

6. To press and stitch the left placket:

• Place the fabric wrong side up, fold along the first set of nips, and press.

• Fold along the second set of nips and press.

• Topstitch the left placket ¼" from the outer fold **(Diagram G)**. (The buttons will hold the facing in place.)

7. Mark the buttonholes on the right front placket **(Diagram H)**.

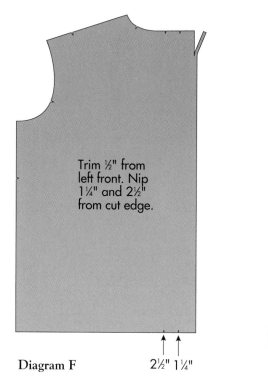

Trim ½" from left front. Nip 1¼" and 2½" from cut edge.

Diagram F   2½" 1¼"

Fold facing along first and second nips. Topstitch ¼" from outer fold.

Diagram G

Mark buttonholes on right front placket.

Diagram H

Note from Nancy: *Use the Pronto Placket on menswear, too. Simply reverse the closure, making the left front for buttonholes and the right front for buttons.*

Space Tape

This see-through tape is perfect for express sewing since it is an automatic buttonhole spacer (the buttonhole placements are the standard 3½" apart). Since you stitch the buttonholes through the tape, the pressure-sensitive tape stabilizes the fabric at the same time. Tear away the excess tape when you're finished.

Space Tape

Hidden Placket

This second technique conceals the button/buttonhole closure for a contemporary look, adding a finished 2"-wide placket. Use a blouse, dress, or shirt pattern that gives the front and the facing as one piece. Modify the pattern to hide the buttons and to give you a palette for decorative stitching. This technique is streamlined in appearance and design—again, only seven simple units!

1. To modify the pattern:

• Trace and cut out a second front pattern piece. (This new pattern will serve as the right front; use the existing pattern as the left front.)

• On the new pattern, cut apart the right front on the fold or the facing line (**Diagram A**).

• Add a ⅝" seam allowance along the pattern front edge (**Diagram B**).

> **Note from Nancy:** *An easy way to add exactly ⅝" is by using a tape measure that is exactly that width. Align one edge of the flat tape along the edge of the blouse pattern and trace along the opposite tape edge. It adds precisely the correct seam allowance needed!*

• Tape a 4⅝" extension to the facing front edge for the placket and the seam allowances. The paper extension should extend above the neckline edge (**Diagram C**).

• Mark vertical lines on the new right front facing pattern at 2", 4", and 4⅝" from the original facing/fold line.

(Continued on page 12)

Hidden Placket

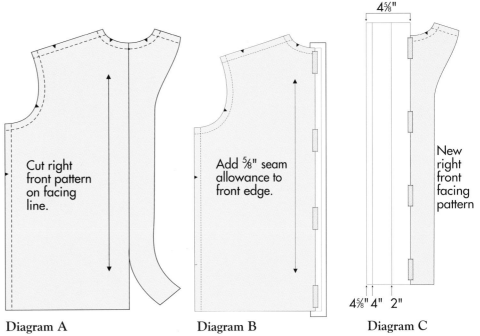

Cut right front pattern on facing line.

Diagram A

Add ⅝" seam allowance to front edge.

Diagram B

4⅝"

New right front facing pattern

4⅝" 4" 2"

Diagram C

Hidden Placket (*continued*)

2. To create the new facing and the neckline shape:

• Fold the facing on the original facing/fold line **(Diagram D, Step 1)**.

• Next, fold back the paper extension on the 2" fold line **(Step 2)**.

• While the paper extension is folded along these lines, trim the neckline, following the cutting line of the original pattern **(Step 3)**.

• Unfold the pattern **(Step 4)**.

3. To cut out the blouse sections:

• Cut the right blouse front and the right facing according to the modified pattern. Mark the fold lines with ¼" nips at the top and the bottom of the pattern.

• Cut out the left blouse front according to the original pattern. (Remember to cut only one each of the left and right blouse fronts.)

4. Fuse the interfacing to both the left and right front facings.

5. To stitch the new right facing to the right front:

• Place right sides together and stitch. Trim and grade the seam allowances. Press flat and then press toward the facing **(Diagram E)**.

• Fold the facing to the inside of the garment along the stitching line. Topstitch 2" from the fold **(Diagram F)**.

> **Note from Nancy:** *For an expressive option, add embroidery stitches to the placket at this point. See page 14,* Add an "Express-ive" Touch.

• Refold the facing toward the outside along the topstitching line. Press **(Diagram G)**.

• Refold the facing toward the inside along the marked line, aligning the facing at the neckline edges and the center fronts. Press **(Diagram H)**.

6. Stitch the left facing to the left front according to the pattern guide sheet.

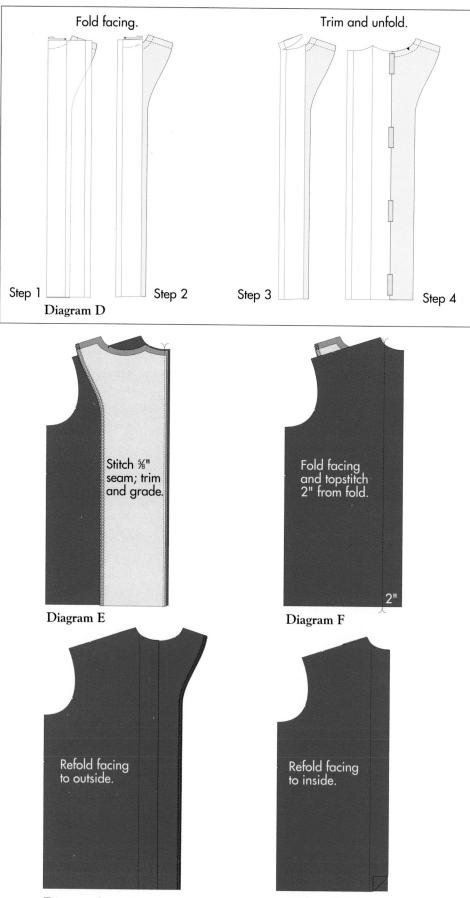

Fold facing.

Trim and unfold.

Step 1   Step 2   Step 3   Step 4

Diagram D

Stitch ⅝"
seam; trim
and grade.

Diagram E

Fold facing
and topstitch
2" from fold.

2"

Diagram F

Refold facing
to outside.

Diagram G

Refold facing
to inside.

Diagram H

7. To finish the neckline:

• With right sides together, stitch the garment fronts to the garment back at the shoulder seams.

• If the pattern has a collar, see page 15, Express Collar, for streamlined directions. Pin the collar to the neckline and stitch before finishing the facing **(Diagram I)**.

• Stitch the back facing to each front facing at the shoulders. Finish the outer facing edge with a zigzag stitch or serge the edge.

• Turn the facing wrong side out. Fold the right front facing on the facing line and the left front facing on the seam; match the notches and pin. Stitch the neck and lower hem facing edges **(Diagram J)**.

• Grade the neck edge seam allowance. Press the seams toward the facing and understitch **(Diagram K)**.

• Grade the hem facing area to ¼".

• Turn the facing to the inside. Tack the facing to the seam allowance **(Diagram L)**.

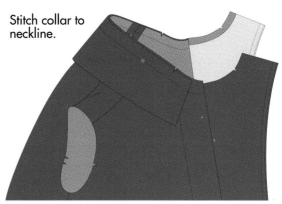

Stitch collar to neckline.

Diagram I

Join facing to blouse at neckline and lower edges.

Diagram J

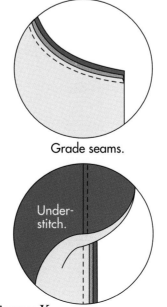

Grade seams.

Understitch.

Diagram K

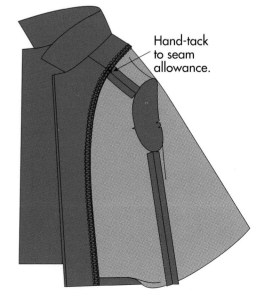

Hand-tack to seam allowance.

Diagram L

*A*dd an "Express-ive" Touch

Express-ive Placket

"Express-ive" is my term for being creative, yet still sewing with streamlined techniques. Sewing express-style doesn't mean forgetting about your creativity. So add your personal style to either placket front with decorative stitching.

Setting up the sewing machine:

1. Use machine embroidery thread in the needle and match the bobbin thread to the fabric.

2. Attach an embroidery or an appliqué foot. Use a foot with a grooved section on the underside to allow the passage of the decorative stitches.

3. Insert a machine embroidery or topstitching needle, size 80 or 90. These needles have longer "eyes" that prevent embroidery threads from shredding, splitting, or breaking.

> **Note from Nancy:** *By loosening the tension, you allow the top thread to slightly wrap to the underside, making the decorative stitch more attractive. After accenting the placket, make certain you put the top tension back to the normal setting for balanced stitches.*

4. Loosen the top tension by two numbers.

5. Back a test sample of fabric with a stabilizer and stitch the design (**Diagram A**).

> **Note from Nancy:** *Make sure the test sample duplicates the number of fabric and interfacing layers used in the garment. This assures your stitching will be the same on the final project.*

6. Determine the design placement on the right front placket between the stitching line and the front edge. Back the placket with a stabilizer and stitch. Remove the stabilizer when finished (**Diagram B**).

"Express-ive" stitching

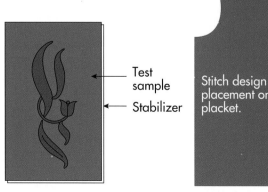

Test sample

Stabilizer

Stitch design placement on placket.

Diagram A

Diagram B

Stitch-N-Tear

A supportive backing for embroidery, **Stitch-N-Tear** *prevents stitches from puckering and slipping. Just place it behind your work, sew the decorative stitches, and then gently tear away the backing.*

$\mathscr{E}$xpress Collar and Collar Band

Express Collar

When you're sewing express-style, this is the collar approach to use. This technique eliminates the bulk from the center front seams and automatically places the under collar on the bias to give the collar greater shape.

1. To create a new collar pattern:

• Cut the pattern apart at the center back **(Diagram A)**.

•Fold under the seam allowance of the center front of one collar and align it with the stitching line of the other collar center front. Pin. Trim the extra triangle shape that forms when the collar sections are overlapped **(Diagram B)**.

• Place waxed paper over the pattern and trace the new collar outline **(Diagram C)**.

• Add a ⅝" seam allowance to one end of the new pattern. Write "Place on fold" at the other end. Cut out the new pattern piece.

• Position the pattern on the fabric fold and cut out the fabric.

> **Note from Nancy:** *If working with a stripe fabric, refold the fabric so that its grain runs horizontally on the upper collar. If you are sewing on a plain fabric, the grain placement is less critical. I have made collars using either grain line, and both placements work fine.*

(Continued on page 16)

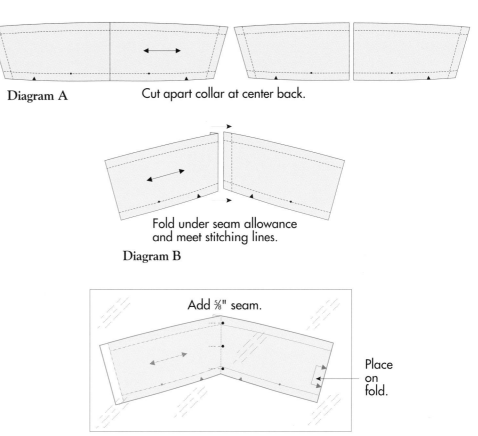

Diagram A   Cut apart collar at center back.

Fold under seam allowance
and meet stitching lines.

Diagram B

Add ⅝" seam.

Place
on
fold.

Diagram C

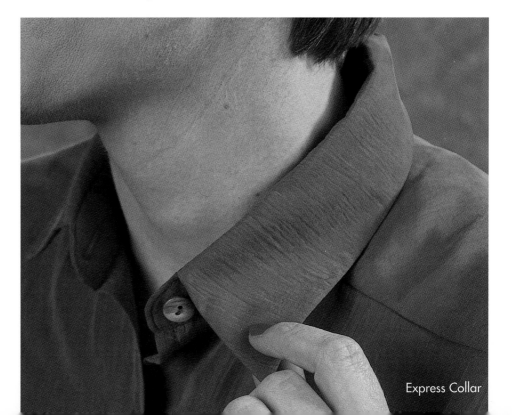

Express Collar

Express Collar *(continued)*

2. To make an interfacing pattern:

• Work on a padded work surface and cover the collar with a length of waxed paper.

• Use a 6" hem gauge with a sliding guide set at ½".

• Guide the end of the point of the seam gauge around the cutting line of the pattern. The gauge will make two lines on the waxed paper: an outer line from the original cutting line and an inner line **(Diagram D)**.

• Use the inner line on the waxed paper as the cutting line for the fusible interfacing. Label the waxed paper pattern and store it in the pattern envelope for future use.

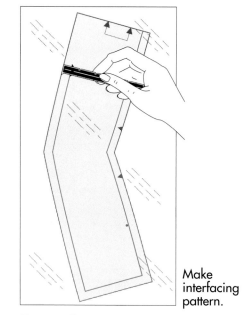

Make interfacing pattern.

Diagram D

> *Note from Nancy: I'll reference these instructions on how to make an interfacing pattern throughout this book. If you haven't tried this technique already, I encourage you to make a sample interfacing pattern so that the method stays in your mind. I frequently make a pattern twice, so I always save my waxed paper interfacing pattern pieces. These patterns are reusable!*

3. Cut out the interfacing and fuse it to the wrong side of the collar **(Diagram E)**.

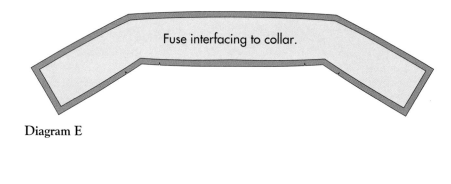

Fuse interfacing to collar.

Diagram E

> *Note from Nancy: There are so many types and weights of fusible interfacings, I recommend that you follow the interleaf (the plastic sheets are sold with the yardage) instructions for fusing. But before fusing, I recommend fusing a test sample. If by chance you have a puckering problem, you'll need to apply pressure. Simply lower your ironing board and lean onto the iron. The added pressure will create a better bond and eliminate the puckering.*

4. Sew the center back seam and press **(Diagram F)**.

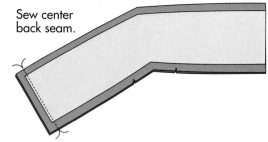

Sew center back seam.

Diagram F

5. To sew the outer edge:
• Refold the collar, with right sides together and the seam placed at the center back **(Diagram G)**.
• Stitch the outer edge.
• Press the seam flat and then open. Grade the seam allowances, trimming the under collar seam to ¼". Trim the collar points on the diagonal to eliminate bulk.

6. Understitch, using a multi-zigzag stitch. Stitch all seam allowances of the under collar to within 1" of the collar points **(Diagram H)**.

7. Turn the collar right side out and press. That's express!

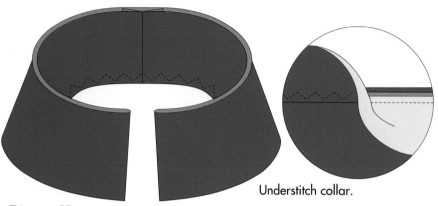

Center seam and stitch outer collar edge.

Diagram G

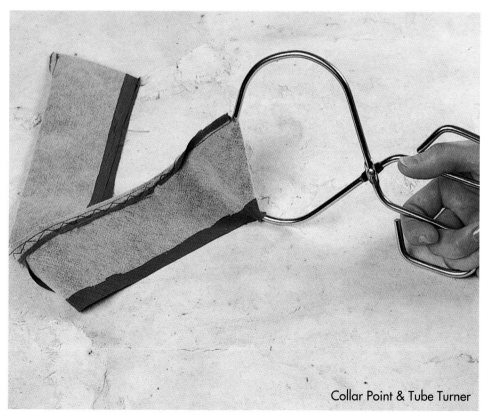

Diagram H

Understitch collar.

Collar Point & Tube Turner
With this tool, you can instantly turn collar and lapel points. Simply place the collar between the scissors-like prongs with the rounded point of the turner on the inside of the collar and turn the collar right side out! The point at the other end of the turner will help form the point of the collar.

Collar Point & Tube Turner

Collar Band

When I first began sewing, I used to avoid patterns with collar bands because the center front curves always had a lump caused by the bulk of the seams. This changed when I learned a bulk-free collar band technique. Combine it with an Express Collar for your next tailored blouse project.

1. To update the pattern pieces:

• Extend the notches toward the seam line.

• Change the neck edge of the front, the back, and the collar band to ¼" seams by trimming ⅜" **(Diagram A)**.

> **Note from Nancy:** *To make sewing easier when joining the outward curve of the collar band neck edge and the inward curve of the blouse neck edge, I work with a ¼" seam. The standard ⅝" seam inhibits these opposite curves from conforming. Keep in mind that ¼" isn't a wide seam. Test your machine for guiding that narrow a seam.*

• Make a nip in the collar bands at the large dots along the collar edge.

2. Cut and fuse interfacing to both collar bands. To make the interfacing piece, see Express Collar on page 15 **(Diagram B)**.

Blouse with collar band

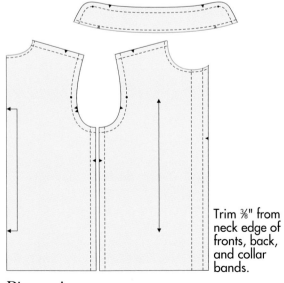

Trim ⅜" from neck edge of fronts, back, and collar bands.

Diagram A

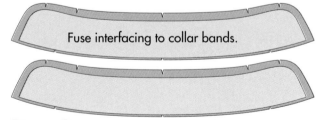

Fuse interfacing to collar bands.

Diagram B

3. Place the collar bands with right sides together and sandwich the neckline in between. Sew the three layers together along the neckline with a ¼" seam (**Diagram C**).

4. To stitch the curve of the collar band:

• Mark with a nip the stopping point for the curved corner.

• Roll the center fronts into a cone shape until the fabric is next to the neckline seam and the collar bands align, with right sides together (**Diagram D**).

•Wrap the neckline seam allowances down toward the inside band.

• Stitch the curve of the collar band from the fold to the nip (**Diagram E**).

• Turn the collar band to the right side and check for accuracy. If it is correct, turn wrong side out and restitch the curve with 18 to 20 stitches per inch.

> **Note from Nancy:** *Whenever stitching curves, I like to shorten the stitch length. The shorter stitches add reinforcement and give me greater accuracy when stitching a curve. Like driving on a curvy road, a reduced speed hugs the curves, making them easier to maneuver.*

5. Clip to the seam allowance at the nip and grade the seams to ⅛".

6. Turn the neck bands right side out and press (**Diagram F**).

7. To attach the collar and finish the collar band:

• Pin the right side of the completed collar (see Express Collar on page 15) to the inner collar band. Stitch with a ⅝" seam (**Diagram G**).

• Press and grade seam allowances.

8. Fold under the outer collar band seam allowance. Pin the outer collar band to the collar and edgestitch around the collar band (**Diagram H**).

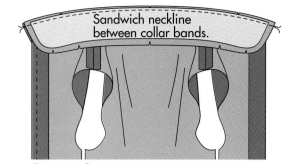
Sandwich neckline between collar bands.
Diagram C

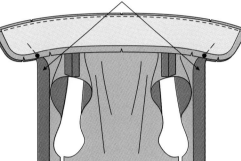
Roll center fronts into cones.
Diagram D

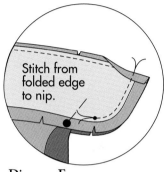
Stitch from folded edge to nip.
Diagram E

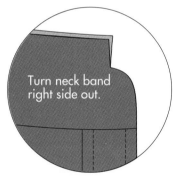
Turn neck band right side out.
Diagram F

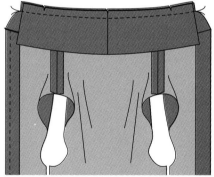
Pin collar to inner collar band and stitch.
Diagram G

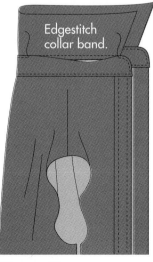
Edgestitch collar band.
Diagram H

Fray Check

If the fabric ravels, secure the clipped edges with a seam sealant such as **Fray Check**. *A small drop of* **Fray Check** *will seal seams and cut edges, and it is completely washable and dry cleanable. You can also lock the ends of serged stitching with a drop of* **Fray Check**.

Sleeve Placket Possibilities

Instant Cuff and Placket

When I think of quickly adding to my wardrobe, I generally think of sewing or serging a knit top. After all, ribbing at the neckline or the sleeves is almost an instant finish. That same instant-finish approach can be applied to a woven fabric cuff on a sleeve. With a quick modification to the pattern, you'll be able to sew a tailored cuff and a sleeve placket with this express-style technique.

1. To make express-style cuff and sleeve modifications:

• Cut a 12½" x 5¼" rectangle to create a new cuff pattern. This measurement fits sizes 8–20 and gives a finished cuff width of 3". Cut two cuffs.

• Measure the bottom width of the sleeve pattern to make sure it exceeds 12½". The extra width allows for the sleeve to be pleated along the lower edge. For example, a 14½" measurement will allow for two ½" pleats.

If your sleeve is narrower than 12½", add strips of waxed paper along the length of each seam allowance. Increase the bottom width by evenly tapering from both sides of the underarm **(Diagram A)**.

• After cutting out the sleeve, transfer the placket marking from the pattern to the right side of the fabric with a washable marking pen or pencil. Do not cut the placket!

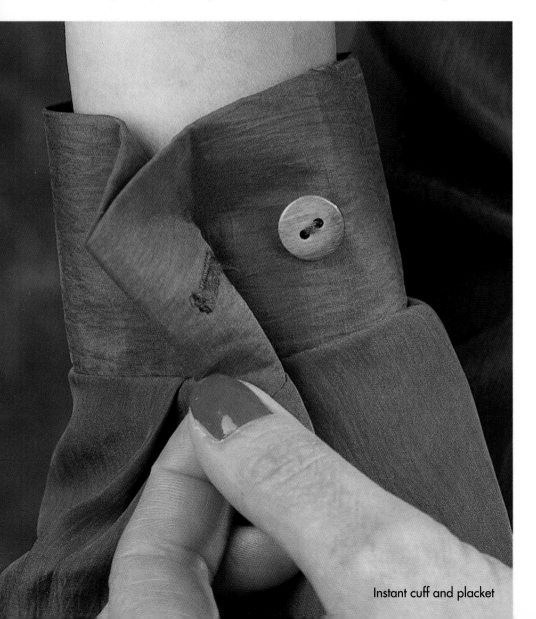

Instant cuff and placket

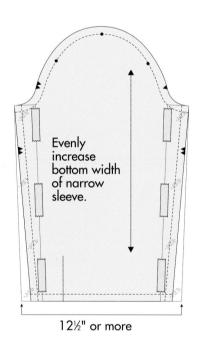

Evenly increase bottom width of narrow sleeve.

12½" or more

Diagram A

2. To fuse interfacing to the cuffs:

• Cut two 11½" x 4½" rectangles from interfacing.

• Position the interfacing on the wrong side of each cuff, ½" from each cut edge. Fuse in place (**Diagram B**).

3. To stitch the cuffs:

• With right sides together, align the short ends of the cuffs and sew into a tube. Press the seam allowance open (**Diagram C**).

• Fold the cuffs in half with wrong sides together and set aside (**Diagram D**).

4. Stitch the sleeve underarm seam. Press.

5. To attach the cuffs to the sleeves:

• If the bottom of the sleeve is wider than the cuff, pleat the lower edge: Form ½" pleats next to the placket until the lower edge of the sleeve meets the cuff size. Create these pleats on the far side of the mark, folding the tucks toward the placket mark (**Diagram E**).

• Pin the cuff to the right side of the sleeve, matching the underarm seams.

6. Sew the cuffs to the sleeves.

• Grade the seam allowances to ¼" and clean-finish the edges by zigzagging, serging, or using Seams Great (**Diagram F**).

• Find the mark on the right side of the fabric indicating the placket area. Crease the cuffs and the sleeves along the placket line (**Diagram G**).

7. Stitch a buttonhole the standard distance (½" to ¾") from each cuff crease, sewing through all layers. Finish the cuffs by sewing on a button.

Note from Nancy: Make a sample buttonhole on a fabric scrap that includes the same number of interfacing layers and fabric folds (four each) to make sure the buttonhole is large enough to accommodate the many layers of fabric.

Position and fuse interfacing to cuff.

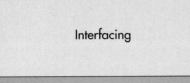

Interfacing

Diagram B

Stitch short ends together and press seam open.

Diagram C

Fold cuff in half, wrong sides together.

Diagram D

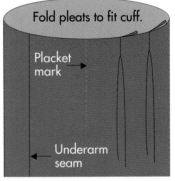

Fold pleats to fit cuff.

Placket mark →

← Underarm seam

Diagram E

Stitch cuff to sleeve.

Diagram F

Crease cuff and sleeve along placket line.

Diagram G

Seams Great

*This ⅝"-wide nylon tricot neatly binds raw edges without causing bulk. Gently pull the **Seams Great** to determine curl direction. Place the raw edge within the curl. While zigzagging in place, gently pull the **Seams Great**. It will automatically curl over the raw edge to be finished. (**Seams Great** is 100% nylon; avoid touching with a hot iron.)*

Express-ive Sleeve Placket

The instant cuff-and-placket tech-nique eliminates the sleeve placket. On the express-ive sleeve placket, however, the placket is the focal point. The de-tail says custom-made. Only you will know how easy it is to sew.

1. To mark the sleeve placket:

• Place a pin on the sleeve fabric to indicate the location for the placket.

• With a fabric marking pen, draw the placket stitching line 1" wide and 4" long for women's wear or 1" wide and 5" long for menswear (**Diagram A**).

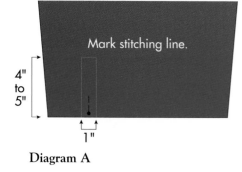

Mark stitching line.

4"
to
5"

1"

Diagram A

"Express-ive" sleeve placket

2. To reinforce the placket:

• Staystitch the placket, stitching around pen lines to provide a stitching guideline **(Diagram B)**.

• Trim the seam allowances within the placket to ¼".

• Clip diagonally to the placket corners and apply Fray Check at the corners to prevent raveling.

3. Cut an 11" x 2½" placket piece for each sleeve. Press under exactly ¼" along one long edge of each placket **(Diagram C)**.

4. To sew the placket piece to the sleeve:

• Spread the placket opening so that the cut edges form a straight line.

• With right sides together, pin the cut edge of the placket to the sleeve placket edge.

• Working from the sleeve side, stitch along the original staystitching, making certain the cut edges of the sleeve and the placket align **(Diagram D)**.

> *Note from Nancy: Stitching the straight portion of the placket is easy, but the fabric folds can get caught in the stitching at the clipped corners. For best results, stitch slowly with a shorter stitch length.*

• Press the seam allowance toward the placket.

• Enclose the seam allowance by wrapping the folded placket edge to the stitching line. Edgestitch along the fold. At the placket's inner corners, stop with the needle in the down position so that it's easier to fold and maneuver the fabric layers **(Diagram E)**.

5. Lap the placket over itself and toward the closest underarm seam. Tuck the corners so that a triangle forms at the top of the placket **(Diagram F)**.

6. Edgestitch the triangular area through all layers **(Diagram G)**.

7. Attach the cuff to the sleeve following the pattern guide sheet.

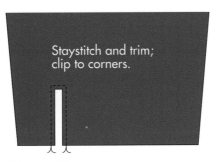

Staystitch and trim; clip to corners.

Diagram B

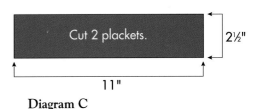

Cut 2 plackets.

2½"

11"

Diagram C

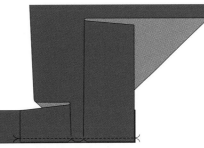

Spread placket opening and stitch to placket.

Diagram D

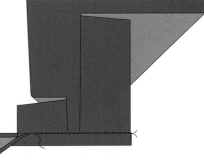

Wrap folded placket edge to stitching line and edgestitch.

Diagram E

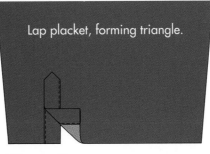

Lap placket, forming triangle.

Diagram F

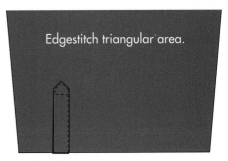

Edgestitch triangular area.

Diagram G

Sleeve Easing Options

Options—that's what I look for in sewing. We have endless fabric, pattern, and style options, so why not experiment with other sewing options! Certain techniques work better and faster than others on specific fabrics.

Sleeve easing is a prime example of a sewing option. Traditionally, we were taught to sew two rows of basting threads and draw the threads to ease the sleeve. This option certainly works, but it can be frustrating when the basting threads break or create a puckered look.

Here are three express-style easing options. Experiment with these choices for the best results in the least amount of time.

Finger Easing

This option requires only one row of stitching between the notches and is perfect for lightweight to medium-weight fabrics. If you have not tried finger easing before, practice on a fabric scrap until you get the feel of the easing step.

1. Adjust the stitching length according to the fabric weight: Use 10 to 12 stitches per inch for medium-weight and 12 to 14 for lightweight.

2. Stitch ½" from the curved edge of the sleeve.

3. Firmly press your finger against the back of the presser foot. Stitch two to three inches, trying to stop the fabric from flowing behind the presser foot; release your finger and repeat. Your finger will prevent the flow of fabric causing the feed dogs to slightly ease each stitch (see photograph).

4. If you have eased too much, simply snip a stitch or two to release some of the gathers. Pull a thread if you need to gather more.

Clear Elastic Easing

Clear Elastic, either ⅜" or ½" wide, is the perfect option for express-easing bulky woven and knit sleeves. See Chapter 2, page 42, for details on easing with clear elastic.

Seams Great Easing

Seams Great, detailed on page 21, can be used to finish seams, but the wider 1¼" width can also be used to ease sleeves on lightweight to medium-weight fabrics. This is the perfect easing option for a beginning sewer.

1. Pin the front and back patterns together at the shoulder seams, stacking the stitching lines. Measure the stitching line from the front notch to the back notch. Cut the 1¼" wide Seams Great the length of the armhole measurement, plus 1" for "handles."

> **Note from Nancy:** *I like to have a ½" "handle" to hold on to while stretching the Seams Great to meet the sleeve. You'll also see I use this same handle idea when easing with Clear Elastic.*

2. Measure ½" from each end and mark with a pin. Also mark the center of the Seams Great. Pin the Seams Great to the wrong side of the sleeve with three pins, matching the raw edges at the notches and the cap.

3. Stretch the Seams Great to meet the sleeve, grasping the handles to help stretch the Seams Great. Sew the two layers together ½" from the cut edge using a regular stitch length. The Seams Great will retract to its original size, automatically causing the sleeve to ease (see photograph).

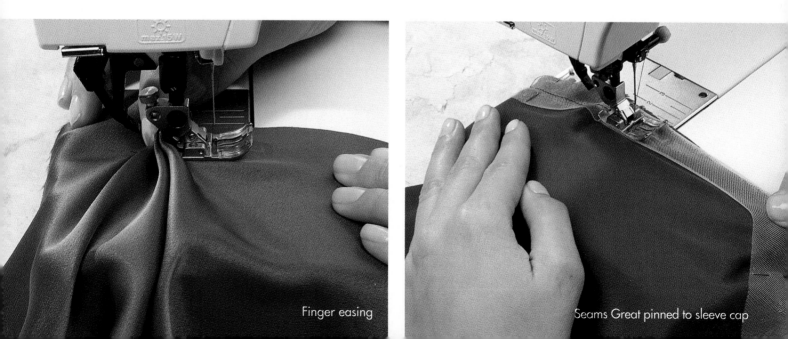

Finger easing

Seams Great pinned to sleeve cap

Gathered Sleeves Staying Power

Sleeve Booster

When your sleeve pattern features pleats or gathers, give the design feature staying power with a sleeve booster. A sleeve booster is a type of a sleeve head sewn into each sleeve of a jacket to keep the gathers or pleats pronounced.

For woven fabrics, use a double layer of organza or bridal illusion (veiling fabric); for knit tops, consider a single layer of polyester fleece.

Creating a sleeve Booster

1. Place a piece of waxed paper or tissue paper over the cap of the sleeve pattern and outline the cap. Measure 2" from the center dot and taper this line to the dots on either side of the sleeve (**Diagram A**).

2. Use the cap pattern to cut the supportive fabrics. Zigzag, serge, or use 5/8"-wide Seams Great to clean-finish the raw edges of the organza or the bridal illusion (**Diagram B**).

3. Pin the sleeve booster fabric to the wrong side of the sleeve. Gather or pleat the sleeve and the sleeve booster as one (see photograph).

4. Set in the sleeve. The added fabric will keep the gathers pronounced, even through washings (see photograph).

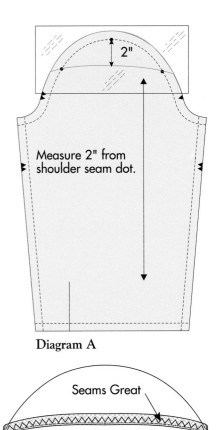

Measure 2" from shoulder seam dot.

2"

Diagram A

Seams Great

Diagram B

Sleeve booster stitched in sleeve

Sleeve with sleeve booster sewn inside

Jackets

A jacket is the perfect piece to build each season's wardrobe around. A lined jacket is comfortable to wear, but it does take many hours to sew. An unlined jacket, on the other hand, takes only a few hours to sew, but it tends to lose its shape in the collar and the shoulder areas. The solution—the Express Jacket!

 Express Jacket Planning

The Express Jacket is a combination of a lined and unlined jacket: the sleeves and the pockets are lined and, to give shaping in the shoulders, the facings of an unlined jacket are extended. With the combined benefits of speed sewing and greater shaping, the Express Jacket will soon be your favorite style.

Express Jacket

Gathering Materials

• Use either a lined or unlined jacket pattern.

Note from Nancy: If you are using a lined jacket pattern, generally the jacket will have a two-piece sleeve and a separate under and upper collar. With an unlined jacket pattern, there will be a one-piece sleeve and one piece for both upper and under collars. My Express Jacket approach to sewing works using either pattern style.

• Purchase 1½ yards of 23"- to 24"-wide fusible interfacing.

• Purchase ¾ yard of lining for the sleeves and the pockets or 1¼ yards if using heavyweight wool or corduroy fashion fabric since the back facing will also be cut from the lining.

Interfacing Sample Sheet

This is a real time-saver when selecting the right interfacing for sewing projects. The guide includes fusible and nonfusible interfacing swatches so you can compare weights with your fashion fabric. Next to each sample is a description of where to use it, the width, the price per yard, and the colors available. Easy-to-follow instructions are included for cutting and fusing interfacing.

Interfacing sample sheets

Fusible Interfacing Guide

	Fabrics	Fusible Interfacings	
Separates and Dresses (Sheer shaping)	voile, chiffon, lawn, gauze, batiste, leno, georgette, dimity, crepe de chine, Charmeuse	Pellon® Fusible #906 Touch O' Gold™	
(Soft shaping)	challis, jersey, single knits, tricot, crepe	Pellon Fusible #911FF Pellon Easy Shaper #114ES Soft 'N Silky	
(Crisp shaping)	shirting, gingham, poplin, chambray, seersucker, cotton, broadcloth, cord, oxford cloth, piqué, lightweight linen, cotton blends, ciré, lightweight denim	Pellon Fusible #931TD Pellon ShirTailor® #950F Stacy® Shape-Flex® #101SF	Armo® Shirt-Shaper™ Shape-up® Lightweight
Coats, Dresses, Jackets, and Suits (Allover shaping)	wool, linen, denim, poplin, corduroy, tweed, flannel, wool blends	Pellon Soft-Shape #880F Armo Fusi-Form™ Lightweight	SuitMaker™ SoftBRUSH™
(Crisp shaping)	gabardine, mohair, synthetic leather, suede	Pellon Pel-aire® #881F Armo Fusi-Form™ Suitweight Armo Form-Flex™ Nonwoven	
Knits Only	double knits, cotton or blended knits, single knits, lightweight sweater knits, terry, jersey, lightweight velour, sweatshirt fleece	Pellon Stretch-Ease™ #921F Stacy Easy Knit™ #130EK Knit Fuse™	SofKNIT™ Quick Knit

Facing Changes

On most lined and unlined jackets, the front and back pieces are both approximately three inches wide at the shoulder seam. For the Express Jacket, the facing pattern pieces are extended into the seam allowances of the sleeves. The extension gives the shoulders greater shape, hides the shoulder pads, and keeps the facings in place.

Making a new front facing:

1. Pin the front facing pattern to the front jacket pattern, matching notches. Place a length of waxed paper or tissue paper over the pattern pieces.

2. With a felt-tip pen, extend the facing's shoulder cutting line to the entire length of the pattern's shoulder seam and then to the center of the armhole **(Diagram A)**.

3. At the center of the armhole, gradually taper the cutting line back to the original facing. Cut out the new front facing pattern.

Making a new back facing:

1. Pin the back facing pattern to the back jacket pattern. Place waxed paper or tissue paper over the pattern pieces.

2. Make the facing shoulder seams the entire length of the jacket back shoulder seam. Extend the facing to the center of the armhole and then across to the center back. Cut out the new back facing pattern **(Diagram B)**.

3. If the pattern has a dart in the shoulder seam, draw the same dart on the back facing pattern. (When constructing the darts, press the facing dart in the opposite direction of the jacket dart.)

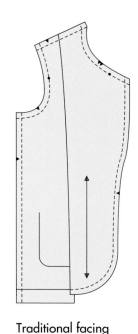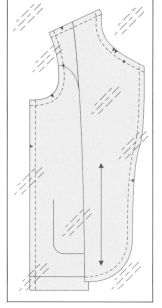

Traditional facing   Extended facing

Diagram A

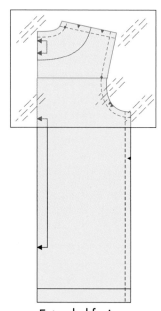

Traditional facing   Extended facing

Diagram B

Interfacing Guidelines

Interfacing gives shape and support to lapels, collar, pocket, hemlines, and shoulder areas. Every fabric piece in an Express Jacket needs interfacing, either full-fuse or partial-fuse.

For full-fuse interfacing:

Follow the guidelines for making interfacing facing patterns on page 16.

1. Fuse the interfacing to the wrong side of the front facings, the back facing, the pockets, the under collar, and the upper collar, extending the interfacing ⅛" into the seam allowances **(Diagram A)**.

2. If the back facing has a dart, remove any interfacing from the dart area.

For partial-fuse interfacing:

Add interfacing to the jacket and sleeve hemlines and the lapel roll line.

1. To shape the roll line, make an interfacing pattern piece as follows:

• Place the edge of the waxed paper ¼" inside the roll line (the diagonal line drawn on the jacket front pattern that starts at the top button and extends into the under collar).

• Use the seam gauge technique on page 16 to mark the interfacing cutting line ⅛" into the seam allowance at the neck and the outer edge of the lapel.

• Mark the interfacing grain line parallel to the jacket grain line.

• Cut the interfacing and position it on the lapel so that it is ¼" from the marked roll line and extends ⅛" into the seam allowances of the other areas of the lapel section.

2. To interface the jacket and sleeve hem allowances:

• For each, cut a bias interfacing strip ¼" wider than the hem allowance.

• Position the interfacing strips with the resin side toward the wrong side of the fabric. Place the strips along the cut edge of the hem allowances, ½" from the side seam cut edges, and fuse **(Diagram C)**.

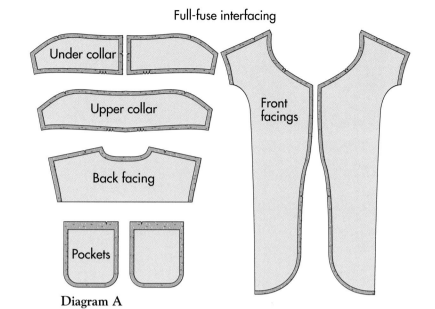

Full-fuse interfacing

Under collar

Upper collar

Back facing

Front facings

Pockets

Diagram A

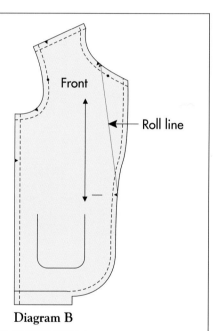

Note from Nancy: I've found an easy way to determine the roll line on the lapel, if it's not marked on the pattern. Extend a line from the top button mark to the center front edge and mark. Locate the notch at the neckline and fold the pattern along a line from the top button mark at the front edge to the neckline notch. This is the roll line. Mark the roll line **(Diagram B)**.

Front

Roll line

Diagram B

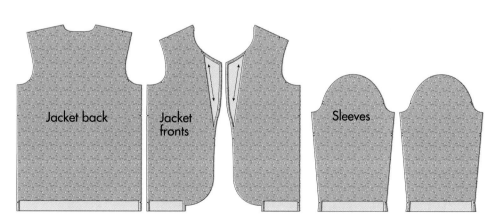

Jacket back

Jacket fronts

Sleeves

Diagram C

Position interfacing on lapel and along hem allowance cut edges, ½" from each side seam cut edge.

Seam and Facing Finishes

When creating an Express Jacket, you can give it a professional look inside and out. Here are two fast seam finishing options and an expressive alternative to try.

Seams Great

Seams Great is a ⅝"-wide nylon fabric that neatly binds a raw edge without causing bulk. It is cut on the bias and will mold around the curves of the outer edge of facings.

To bind a seam, place the raw edge of the fabric within the "curl" of the Seams Great. Straightstitch or zigzag in place (**Diagram A**).

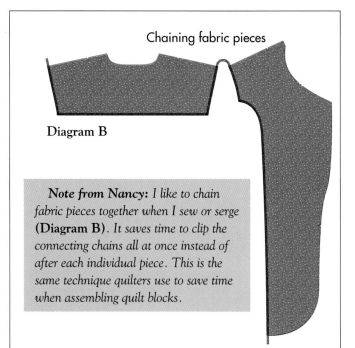

Chaining fabric pieces

Diagram B

Note from Nancy: *I like to chain fabric pieces together when I sew or serge* (**Diagram B**). *It saves time to clip the connecting chains all at once instead of after each individual piece. This is the same technique quilters use to save time when assembling quilt blocks.*

Finish raw edge with Seams Great.

Diagram A

Serging

Serge the raw edge by using a two- or three-thread overedge stitch.

An Express-ive Finish

For an express-ive finish, cut bias strips from a lightweight blouse or dress fabric and finish the seams with a creative touch.

1. Cut 1"-wide bias strips from lightweight fabric that coordinates with the jacket fabric.

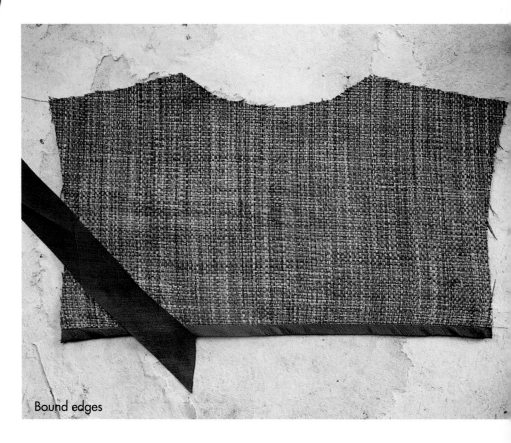

Bound edges

2. With right sides together and raw edges aligned, place the bias strips on the facing or seam edge. Stitch using a ¼" seam.

3. Wrap the bias strip around the raw edge to the underside of the fabric. It's not necessary to finish the unsewn edge of the strip, as the bias edge will not ravel.

4. Stitch in-the-ditch to catch the underside of the strip **(Diagram C)**.

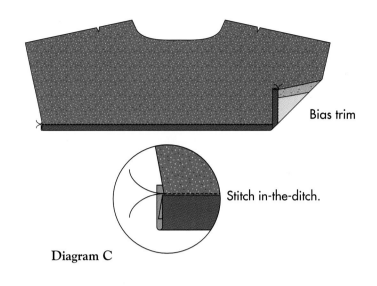

Bias trim

Stitch in-the-ditch.

Diagram C

> *Note from Nancy: "Stitch in-the-ditch" is one of those coined phrases that if taken out of context could be extremely confusing! It means to stitch from the right side in the groove or "ditch" of the seam. The stitching line is hidden in the seam, yet catches the underside of the fabric. You'll find many other areas where stitching in-the-ditch is an express-style step.*

ThreadFuse

ThreadFuse

ThreadFuse, a two-ply thread containing a heat-activated fusible nylon filament, is an express-style thread. It is perfect for streamlining your sewing process when adding bias trim. Wind **ThreadFuse** *on the bobbin and use regular thread in the top. With the wrong side of the facing down, stitch using a ¼" seam. Wrap the bias strip over the edge and press. The* **Thread-Fuse** *will hold the bias strip in place, making it easier to edgestitch. Change back to regular bobbin thread and stitch in-the-ditch to catch the underside of the strip.*

Lined Patch Pocket

Express sewing is fast sewing but also smart sewing. This next technique is the fastest way I know to sew a lined pocket, and it is smart because the lining provides greater shape and prevents the pocket from sagging.

1. To cut the pocket lining:
• Fold under the top hem allowance of the pattern to create the pocket lining pattern **(Diagram A)**.
• Cut the lining on the bias to avoid excess raveling.

2. To stitch the lining to the pocket:
• With right sides together, align the hemline edges of the pocket fabric and the lining.

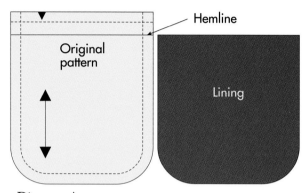

Hemline

Original
pattern

Lining

Diagram A

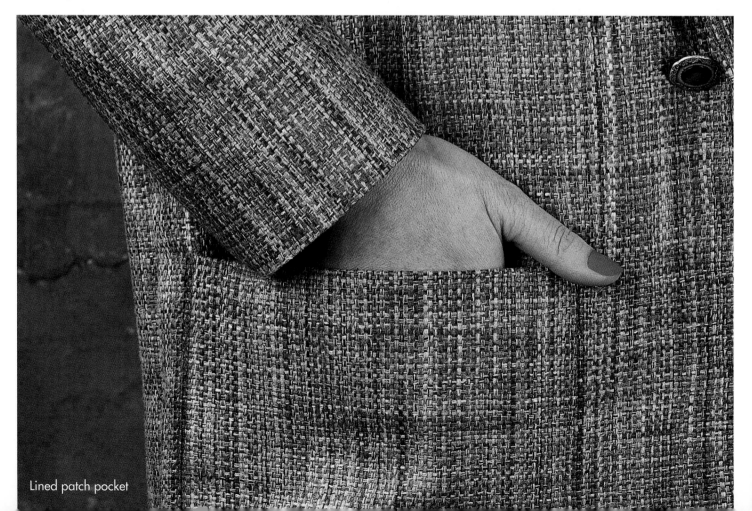

Lined patch pocket

• Stitch along the hem allowance using a ⅝" seam. Press the seam allowance flat and then toward lining.

3. To press the outer pocket to the finished size:

• Press under ⅝" on the sides and the lower edge of the pocket using a piece of cardboard cut to the finished pocket size, a Pocket Curve Template, or a hem gauge (**Diagram B**).

• If the fabric is bulky, trim the seam allowance around the corners to ⅜".

4. To position the lining section of the pocket on the jacket:

• Align the markings on the pocket with the markings on the jacket. Flip up the outer pocket and pin the lining to the jacket.

• Mark 1" seam allowance on the lining (**Diagram C**).

5. To stitch the lining section of the pocket to the jacket:

• Set your machine for a medium zigzag stitch.

• Begin sewing at the pocket top using a ⅝" seam and gradually increase the seam allowance to 1" as you reach the lining.

• Sew the lining along the 1" seam allowance.

• Taper back to a ⅝" seam allowance on the second side of pocket top (**Diagram D**).

(Continued on page 36)

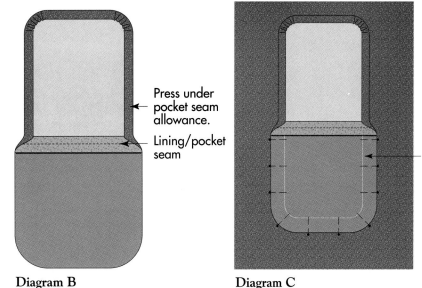

Press under pocket seam allowance.

Lining/pocket seam

Diagram B

1" seam allowance

Diagram C

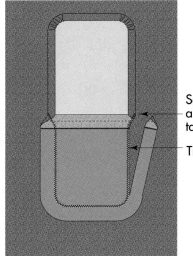

Sew 1" seam allowance, tapering to ⅝".

Trim.

Diagram D

Pocket Curve Template

*I can swiftly and accurately press seam allowances and mold corners on pockets with the **Pocket Curve Template.** The template has four different corner shapes. Simply place the desired template curve on the seam line of the pocket and mold the seam allowance over the template. Attach the clip section to hold the pocket in place. Press.*

Pocket Curve Template

Lined Patch Pocket (*continued*)

6. To trim excess seam allowance from the lining:

• Use appliqué scissors or bevel your scissors and cut with the blades parallel to the fabric.

• Zigzag over the first few stitches for reinforcement.

7. To topstitch the outer pocket:

• Turn down the outer pocket over the lining.

• Topstitch the pocket in place by edgestitching around the pocket edge **(Diagram E)**.

• Or blindhem-stitch the pocket in place to give the pocket a handstitched look (see photograph).

—Attach a blindhem foot. With nylon or monofilament thread in the top of the machine and matching thread in the bobbin, adjust the blindhem stitch to a medium width and length.

—Stitch from the right side with straight stitches in-the-ditch between the pocket and the jacket, with the "zag" barely catching the pocket edge.

Turn pocket down and topstitch.

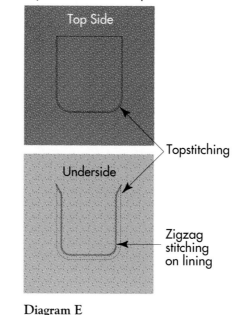

Diagram E

Appliqué Scissors

Appliqué scissors are indispensable when trimming excess fabric. The pelican-shaped bill of this scissors makes it easier to trim the excess fabric close to a line of stitching without nicking the fabric. Position the rounded blade under the fabric and the trim.

Wonder Thread

Wonder Thread, a nylon monofilament thread, is the perfect thread for the blindhem stitch. It is available in either clear or smoke and blends with almost any fabric.

Blindhem stitch using Wonder Thread.

Wrapped Corners on Collar and Lapels

When sewing an Express Jacket, use the wrapped corner to save time and eliminate bulk from the collar and the lapel. Jacket patterns may have separate pattern pieces for the upper and under collar or may combine both into one piece. The express wrapped corner technique works with either pattern style and can be serged on an overlock machine or stitched on a conventional machine.

1. Fuse interfacing to both the upper and under collars. (See Express Collar, page 15.)

2. To stitch the outer edges of the collars together:

• With right sides together and raw edges aligned, pin the collars along the outer seam.

• Stitch the outer seam. Press the seam flat and then open.

• Grade the seam allowance, with the under collar trimmed to ¼" and the upper collar to ⅜" **(Diagram A)**.

3. Press the seam toward the under collar; understitch **(Diagram B)**.

(Continued on page 38)

Wrapped corner on collar and lapel

Grade seam allowance.

Diagram A

Understitch collar.

Diagram B

Wrapped Corners (*continued*)

4. To stitch the collar front edges:
• Fold the collar along the front edge stitching line (the seam automatically wraps toward the under collar).

> **Note from Nancy:** *The great advantage of my wrapped corner technique is that it allows you to understitch the entire outer edge, something not possible with the traditional collar technique.*

• Sew the center front seam from the fold to the edge. Repeat on the other end.
• Grade the seam allowances and cut the corners at an angle. Press the seams flat and then open (**Diagram C**).
• Turn the collar right side out. Press.
5. To join collar to jacket:
• With right sides together, align raw edges of fronts and back jacket sections at shoulder seams and stitch. Press seams flat and then open.
• Meet under collar to right side of jacket back at neckline.
• Machine-baste the collar to the neckline using a ½" seam allowance (**Diagram D**).

> **Note from Nancy:** *When you have problems with the fabric being pulled into the feed dogs or if the thread knots when you begin to stitch, use a folded scrap of fabric called an anchor cloth. Sew a few stitches in the anchor cloth, butt the fabric up to the anchor cloth, and continue sewing. After the seam is sewn, simply snip the threads between the anchor cloth and the seam.*

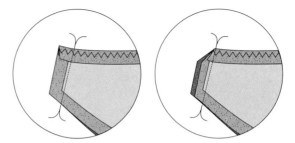

Sew center front seam, grade, and clip corner.
Diagram C

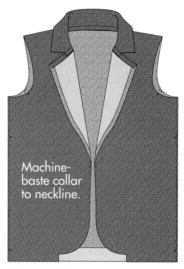

Machine-baste collar to neckline.

Diagram D

Anchor cloth

6. To join facings to jacket:

• With right sides together, pin front facing to back facing at the shoulders and stitch. Press seams flat and then open (**Diagram E**).

• With right sides together and raw edges aligned, pin the facing piece to the jacket neckline, with the collar sandwiched in between, and stitch. Press the seam flat and then open (**Diagram F**).

• Grade the seam allowance, with the facing edge being the smallest.

• Press the seam allowance toward the facing and understitch only between the shoulder seams of the back facing (**Diagram G**).

7. To stitch the lapel corner:

• At the lapel corner, wrap the neckline seam allowance toward the jacket side (**Diagram H**). The neckline stitching line will be at the fold. Pin.

• Pin the facing to the jacket along the center edges, matching notches. The facing is generally ¼" longer than the jacket front, so the facing will fit smoothly as it becomes the turned-back lapel.

• With the jacket side up, stitch the front seam.

• Press the seam flat and then open. Grade and angle-cut the bulk from the lapel point as illustrated (**Diagram I**).

• Clip to the stitching line at the end of the roll line (across from the top buttonhole position).

• Grade the jacket front shorter than the front facing *above* the clip.

• Grade the front facing shorter than the jacket front *below* the clip (**Diagram J**).

• Press the seam allowance below the clip toward the facing and understitch.

• Press the seam allowance above the clip toward the jacket front and then understitch.

8. Turn the collar and the lapel right side out and press.

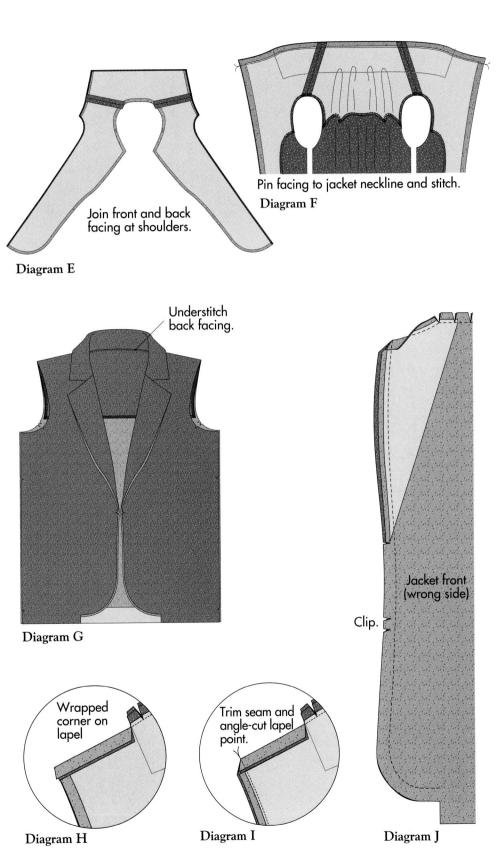

Join front and back facing at shoulders.

Diagram E

Pin facing to jacket neckline and stitch.

Diagram F

Understitch back facing.

Diagram G

Wrapped corner on lapel

Diagram H

Trim seam and angle-cut lapel point.

Diagram I

Jacket front (wrong side)

Clip.

Diagram J

Lined Sleeves—Express Style!

It's a snap to stitch a lined sleeve with the following technique! It doesn't take any more time than sewing an unlined sleeve, yet it automatically hems the sleeve and acts as an accent when the sleeve is turned back to show off a contrasting lining. The lining gives the sleeve additional body and makes it easier to slip on over a blouse or a sweater.

Lined sleeves

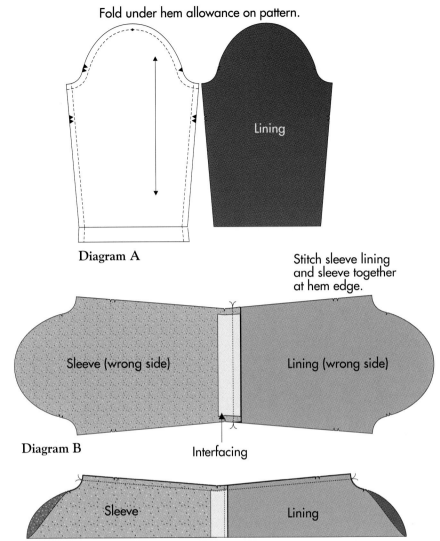

Fold under hem allowance on pattern.

Lining

Diagram A

Note from Nancy: *This express-style sleeve is lined and hemmed at the same time, so it is important that the sleeve pattern is altered to the correct length prior to cutting. Double-check your arm length against the pattern's sleeve length and make any needed changes.*

1. To cut the lining:

• Fold under the hem allowance on the sleeve pattern to create the lining pattern.

• Cut out the lining **(Diagram A)**.

2. To join the sleeve and the lining at the hem edge:

• With right sides together, align the hem edges of the sleeve and the sleeve lining and pin. Stitch using a ⅝" seam **(Diagram B)**.

3. Grade the hem seam allowance, with the lining seam being the smallest. Press the seam flat and then towards the lining.

4. To stitch the underarm seam:

• Align and pin the underarm seams of the lining and the sleeve.

• Stitch the entire underarm seam. Press the seam flat and then open **(Diagram C)**.

(Continued on page 42)

Stitch sleeve lining and sleeve together at hem edge.

Sleeve (wrong side)   Lining (wrong side)

Diagram B   Interfacing

Sleeve   Lining

Diagram C   Stitch underarm seam.

Seam Stick

*Press the sleeve seams over a **Seam Stick** or a **seam roll,** which is flat on one side so it does not roll. The rounded surface will aid you in pressing a seam flat without imprinting unsightly seam edges on the right side of the fabric.*

Seam Stick

Lined Sleeves (*continued*)

5. To complete the sleeve lining:

• Reach inside the sleeve, grasp the fashion fabric and the lining at the hemline, and pull right side out.

• Align the raw edges of the sleeve and the lining at the sleeve cap (**Diagram D**).

• Smooth the sleeve hem and press.

• Zigzag or serge sleeve caps together and handle the two sleeve layers as one.

6. Ease the fullness in the sleeve cap using Clear Elastic.

> **Note from Nancy:** *I've found Clear Elastic, either ⅜"- or ½"-wide, is the perfect option for express-easing bulky woven and knit sleeves. I used ½"-wide Clear Elastic for easing the lined wool jacket sleeve of the Express Jacket. The results were phenomenal. The sleeve fit perfectly into the armhole! (For lightweight fabrics, see Sleeve Easing Options on page 24.)*

• Pin the front and back patterns together at the shoulder seam, stacking the stitching lines. Measure the length of the jacket armhole along the seam line, from the front notch and across the shoulder to the back notch (**Diagram E**).

• Cut the Clear Elastic the length of the armhole measurement plus 1" for "handles."

• Measure ½" from each end and mark with a ballpoint pen. Fold the elastic in half and mark the center. Also mark the positions for the top of the sleeve cap (shoulder) and the sleeve dots (**Diagram F**).

• Set your machine to a medium stitch length.

Meet raw edges of sleeve and lining at sleeve cap. Zigzag or serge sleeve caps together.

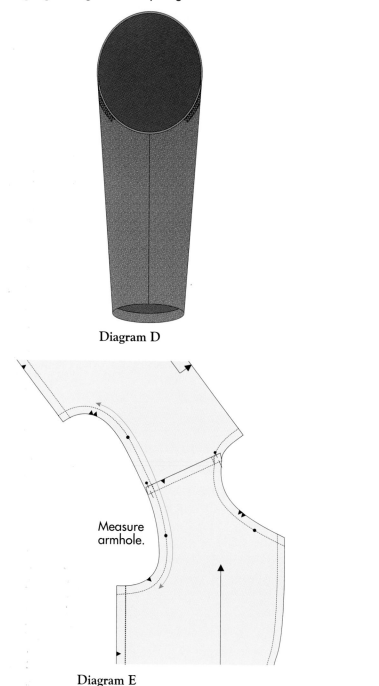

Diagram D

Measure armhole.

Diagram E

Handle		Sleeve dot		Shoulder		Sleeve dot		Handle
½"	⁄ ⁄	⁄ ⁄	⁄ ⁄	⁄ ⁄	⁄ ⁄	⁄ ⁄	⁄ ⁄	½"

Diagram F   Mark clear elastic.

• With the elastic on the wrong side of the fabric, align the marks on the elastic with the notches and the dots at the cap of the sleeve (**Diagram G**).

• Sew a few stitches at one sleeve notch to anchor the elastic to the sleeve. Stretch the elastic to meet the sleeve and stitch, beginning and ending at the ⅝" mark and using the handle to stretch the elastic.

• Keep the elastic in the sleeve, as it doesn't cause any bulk (**Diagram H**).

7. To set in the sleeve:

• With right sides together, pin the sleeve to the armhole, matching the notches, the underarm seams, and the cap dot to the shoulder seam.

• Stitch the armhole. Using a ⅜" seam, restitch the underarm area between the notches for reinforcement.

• Trim the armhole underarm seam allowance between the notches (**Diagram I**).

• Press the armhole seam allowance flat. Press the seam toward the sleeve after sewing in a sleeve head. (See Sleeve Head, page 46.)

Note from Nancy: *To fill out the fullness in the cap of the sleeve, I like to insert a sleeve head. By waiting to press the seam toward the sleeve after the sleeve head is in place, you'll prevent wrinkles from being pressed into the sleeve.*

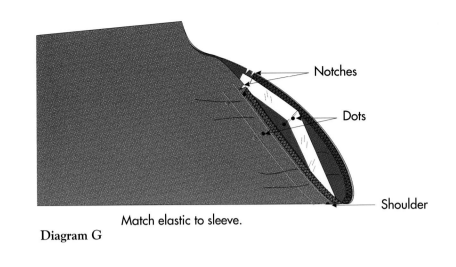

Match elastic to sleeve.

Diagram G

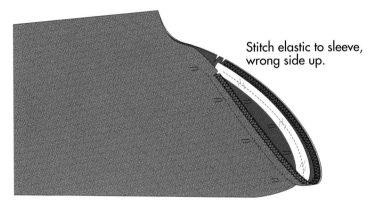

Stitch elastic to sleeve, wrong side up.

Diagram H

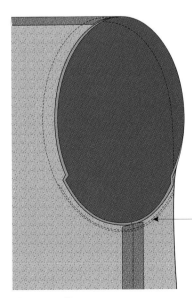

Restitch underarm area. Trim between notches.

Diagram I

*T*wo-Piece Sleeve with Vent

If your two-piece sleeve doesn't have a vent, give the illusion of a vent with the following express-ive technique. It's a great shortcut!

1. To cut and stitch the lining:

• Fold under the hem and fold in the vent extension on both the upper and under sleeve pattern pieces (**Diagram A**).

• Cut out the lining pieces.

• Pin the upper and under sleeve linings at the front seam, with right sides together and raw edges aligned, stretching the upper sleeve to fit between the notches. Stitch.

• Press the seam open over a seam roll.

2. To apply interfacing to the sleeve hem and the vent sections:

• Cut several bias strips of interfacing the width of the hem plus ⅛". For the sleeve vents, cut the strips the width of the vent plus ⅛".

• Place the bias strips, resin side to the wrong side of the sleeve, along the edges of the hem and the vent allowances. Begin and end the placement ½" from the cut edges of the seam to minimize bulk (**Diagram B**).

3. Stitch the front seams of the upper and under sleeves, with right sides together and raw edges aligned. Press the seam open over a seam roll. Trim the seam within the hem allowance (**Diagram C**).

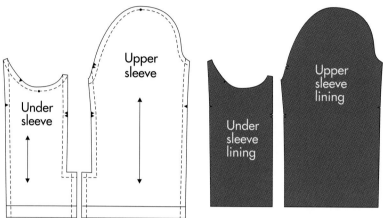

For 2-piece sleeve lining, fold up hem; fold in vent extensions.

Diagram A

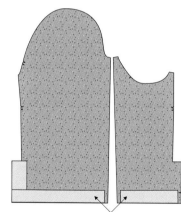

Extend interfacing ⅛" into the seam allowance.

Diagram B   Interfacing

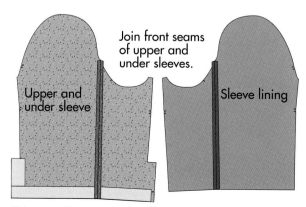

Join front seams of upper and under sleeves.

Diagram C

4. With right sides together, align the lower edges of the sleeve and the lining. Stitch together using a ⅝" seam. Press the seam flat and then press toward the lining (**Diagram D**).

5. With raw edges aligned, refold and stitch the back seam, leaving the vent section between the dots unstitched.

• Clip the under sleeve seam allowance above and below the vent seam.

• Stitch the vent extensions together near the cut edge (**Diagram E**).

6. Press the sleeve and lining seams open. Press the vent toward the upper sleeve (**Diagram F**).

7. Reach inside the fashion fabric sleeve, grasp the fashion fabric and the lining at the hemline, and pull right side out. Adjust the hem with your fingers until the vent lies flat. Finish following the steps for a one-piece sleeve.

Note from Nancy: When the sleeves are finished, sew two to three buttons in each vent area. I like this express-ive style sleeve because I don't need to stitch buttonholes.

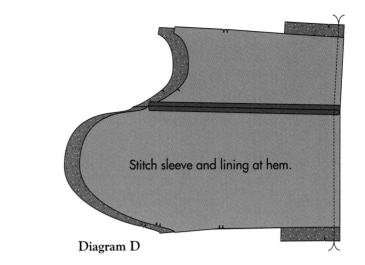

Stitch sleeve and lining at hem.

Diagram D

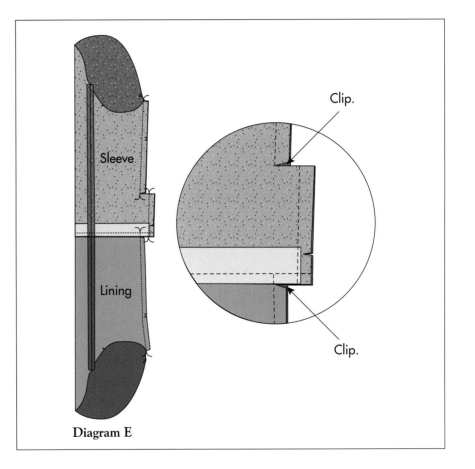

Clip.

Sleeve

Lining

Clip.

Diagram E

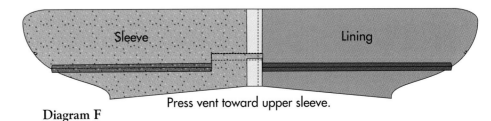

Sleeve

Lining

Press vent toward upper sleeve.

Diagram F

Sleeve Head

After the sleeve is set in the jacket, insert a sleeve head—a small strip of fleece that helps fill out the fullness of the cap—for a softer and more professional appearance.

1. Cut two 1½" x 10" strips of polyester fleece. Fold each strip in half, short ends together, and mark the center.

2. Align the raw edges of the sleeve cap and the straight edge of the sleeve head. Match the center mark with the shoulder seam and pin (**Diagram A**).

3. From the jacket side of the armhole, stitch the sleeve head in place, sewing over the previous stitching.

4. With the wrong side out, press the seams over a dressmaker's ham. Press the seam allowances and the sleeve head toward the sleeve (**Diagram B**).

Note from Nancy: A sleeve head is one of those small but crucial jacket elements. Without the sleeve head, the extra ease from the sleeve has no place to go and frequently the sleeve appears as if it has no shape.

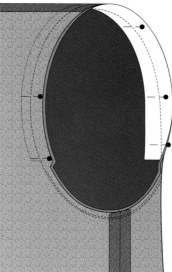

Pin sleeve head to sleeve side of armhole.

Diagram A

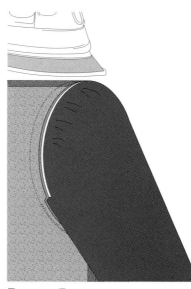

Press seams from underside over dressmaker's ham.

Diagram B

Custom-made Shoulder Pads

Shoulder pads give a special finishing touch to the shoulder and sleeve area and make your jacket hang straight down from the shoulders for a flattering look. You can purchase shoulder pads, but it's easy and economical to make your own. By tracing the shoulder shape of the front and back pattern pieces, you can make a pair of shoulder pads that custom fit the shape of the jacket.

1. To prepare the pattern:
• Stack the shoulder stitching lines of the front and back pattern pieces.
• Place three sheets of waxed paper over the shoulder area.
• Trace the armhole cutting line with a dull pencil or a tracing wheel **(Diagram A)**.

2. To draw the shoulder pad shapes:
• Place a pin at the armhole edge of the shoulder seam cutting line. Tape thread or string to a felt-tip pen; wind the other end around the pin several times until the length of the thread between the pin and the pen point is 5".
• Draw an arc, beginning and ending at the armhole edges **(Diagram B)**.
• Move the pen in 1" toward the armhole edges and wind the thread around the pin until taut.
• Draw a second arc, 1" smaller than the previous arc.
• Move the pen in 1" and repeat to complete the third arc **(Diagram C)**.

(Continued on page 48)

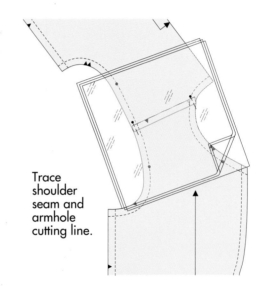

Trace shoulder seam and armhole cutting line.

Diagram A

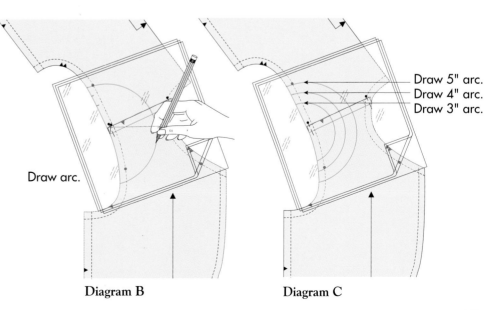

Draw arc.

Diagram B

Draw 5" arc.
Draw 4" arc.
Draw 3" arc.

Diagram C

Shoulder Pads (*continued*)

3. To cut the shapes:
 • Cut four layers of fusible interfacing using the largest arc pattern.
 • Cut two layers each of thick fusible
craft fleece using the two smaller arc
patterns.
 • Make nips on all the pads at the
inner and outer shoulder seams for easy
alignment **(Diagram D)**.

> *Note from Nancy: The thickness of
> the shoulder pads depends upon style and
> personal preference. If you would like
> thicker pads, simply cut more layers of
> the fleece and custom-make this shoulder
> shaping to your needs.*

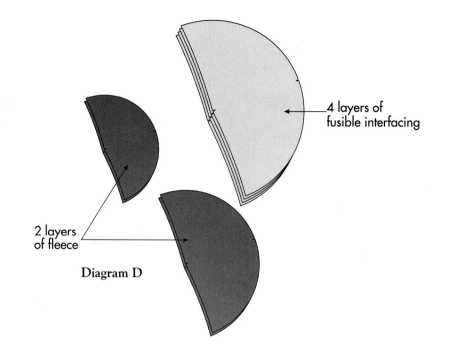

4 layers of
fusible interfacing

2 layers
of fleece

Diagram D

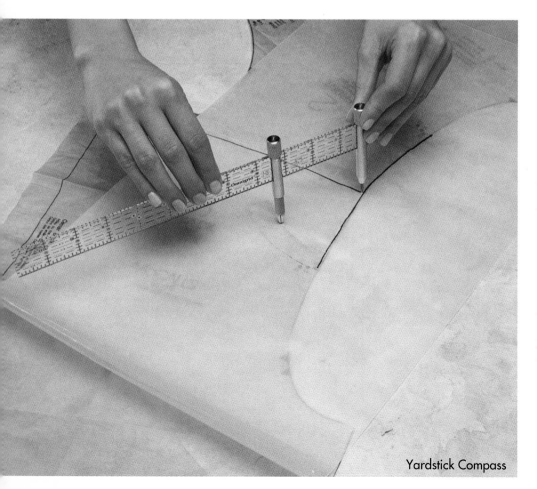

Yardstick Compass

*Using a **Yardstick Compass**
is the quickest way to draw the
arc shapes. Insert a 12″ ruler
between the components of the
Yardstick Compass. Make
the space between the pointed
end of the compass and the
end of the pencil equal the
length of the shoulder seam
(minus the seam allowances).
Draw the two smaller arcs in
the same manner, moving the
pen to decrease the space 1″
each time.*

Yardstick Compass

4. To make one shoulder pad:

• Stand a pressing ham on its side. Place one layer of fusible interfacing on it, fusible side up.

• Center a piece of the smallest arc of fleece on top of the fusible layer; then center the remaining arc of fleece over the smallest piece, matching nips.

• Top the layers with a layer of fusible interfacing, fusible side down.

• Place pins along the center of the shoulder pad and smooth the layers around the pressing ham so that the shoulder pad conforms to the ham.

• Trim the interfacing pieces so that they are the same length.

5. To fuse all the layers together:

• Set your steam iron on a wool setting and steam-baste the layers.

• Cover the shoulder pad with a press cloth and fuse.

(Continued on page 50)

Conforming

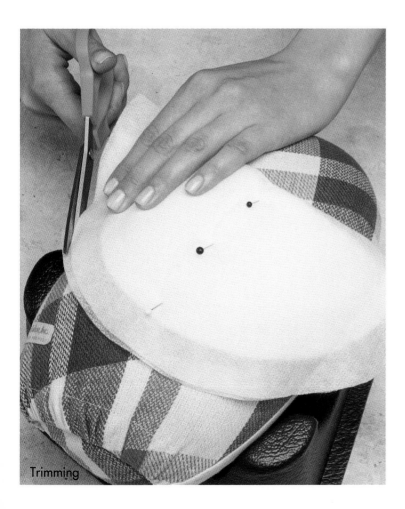

Trimming

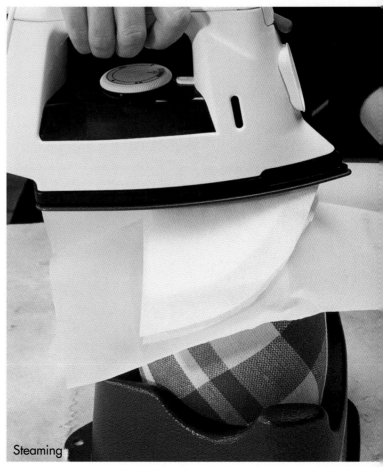

Steaming

49

Shoulder Pads (*continued*)

6. Serge or zigzag the layers together along the edges **(Diagram E)**.

7. To tack a shoulder pad in an armhole:

• Pin the shoulder pad in the jacket, matching the raw edges of the pad to the raw edges of the armhole seam allowance.

• Tack the shoulder pad to the seam allowance at the cap, the center armhole dots, and the neck edge **(Diagram F)**.

> *Note from Nancy:* I always tack thread shanks within the seam allowance, sewing shanks by hand (as with buttons) or by bar-tacking by machine using a fringe or tailor tack foot. I've found a thread shank is necessary to prevent pulling and dimpling on the right side of the jacket. When using the fringe or tailor tack foot, I set the machine at the widest bar-tack setting. As the thread sews over the high center bar of the foot, it will create a shank.

8. Cover the shoulder pads with the extended facings and pin. Attach the facing at intervals to the armhole seam allowance, using hand-sewn tacks or machine-sewn bar tacks **(Diagram G)**.

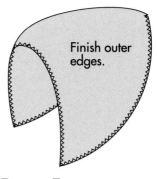

Diagram E

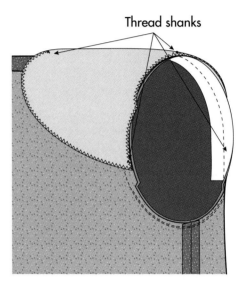

Diagram F

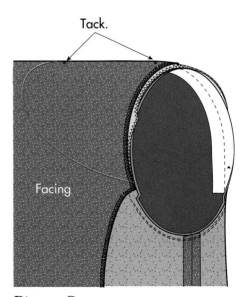

Diagram G

Topstitching Tips

A final detail in sewing a jacket is topstitching around the lapel and the collar. Topstitching is optional, but it adds another custom accent and enhances the stability of the edges.

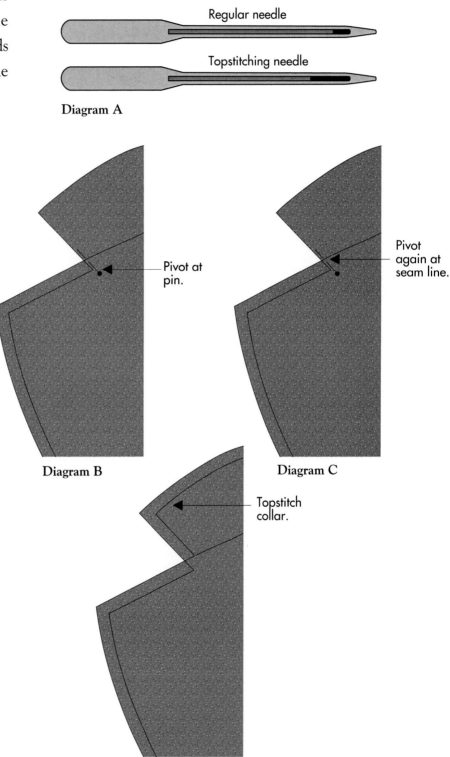

Diagram A

Pivot at pin.

Pivot again at seam line.

Diagram B

Diagram C

Topstitch collar.

Diagram D

- Use double threads in both the top and the bobbin to give a more balanced tension to your topstitching. If your machine does not have two spool spindles, wind two bobbins and stack them on top of each other on the thread spindle. Thread them through the guides as if they were one thread. Wind the thread for the bobbin with two threads at the same time.
- Use a topstitching needle or a machine embroidery needle with an extra large eye to accommodate the two threads (**Diagram A**).
- Lengthen the stitch length slightly to approximately eight stitches per inch and adjust the needle and bobbin tensions.
- Place a pin parallel to the point where the collar joins the lapel (lapel point). Stitch from the bottom hem edge to the pin and stop with the needle in the fabric. Pivot and sew to the lapel point (**Diagram B**).
- Pivot and sew two or three stitches in the collar seam (**Diagram C**).
- Pivot and continue to topstitch around the collar (**Diagram D**).

Skirts & Pants

Skirts and pants are both essential to completing a wardrobe and can be sewn express-style using streamlined sewing techniques. But don't think just because your sewing is streamlined you have to forget about adding details. You will be delighted to discover how fast—and express-ive—it is to sew skirts and pants to fill out your wardrobe!

Skirts—Express Style!

Express Skirt—30 Minutes or Less!

When your wardrobe needs an update, the Express Skirt is the answer. Make it short, long, slim, or full; any which way you make it, you'll only need 30 minutes or so.

1. To determine the amount of fabric and Stitch 'n Stretch needed:

• For most sizes, one length of 54"- or 60"-wide fabric is all that you need.

• For a straight skirt, cut a fabric rectangle:

— Width: measure the hip and add 5" for ease.

— Length: determine the finished length and add 2½" for the hems.

• For a full skirt, cut a fabric rectangle:

— Width: measure the hip and add 10" or more.

— Length: determine the finished length and add 2½" for the hems.

• Cut Stitch 'n Stretch elastic the same width as the skirt.

2. To prepare the fabric and the elastic:

• Clean-finish the raw edges of the side seams if using a woven fabric.

• Press under ½" at the top of the skirt.

• Pull out the spandex cords ½" from each end of the woven band. The free ends of the cords will be the "handles" for pulling the cords.

• Fold under the short ends of the woven band.

3. Pin the woven band ⅛" from the top fold on the wrong side of the fabric (**Diagram A**).

Stitch 'n Stretch Waistband

Note from Nancy: *Elastics are generally cut smaller than the waistband; Stitch 'n Stretch is the exception to the rule. Always allow a one-to-one ratio of fabric to elastic with this specialty elastic.*

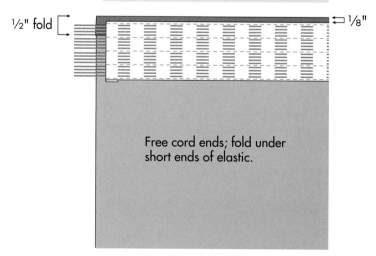

½" fold ⟶ ⟵ ⅛"

Free cord ends; fold under short ends of elastic.

Diagram A

4. To stitch the woven band and adjust the cords:

• Stitch the woven band to the skirt along each of the blue stitching lines or along white stitching lines on black Stitch 'n Stretch (**Diagram B**).

• Pull the elastic cords equally from both ends to fit the waistline (**Diagram C**). Baste the seam partially closed and try on the skirt. Adjust the elastic cords as needed.

(Continued on page 56)

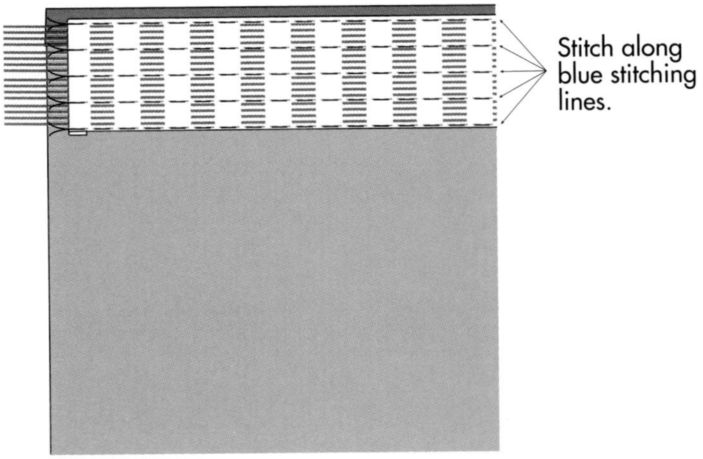

Note from Nancy: *To evenly gather the Stitch 'n Stretch, gently pull the elastic cords out 4" to 5" at one end and tie the cords into a knot. Pull the elastic cords until you have gathered half of the skirt. Repeat for the second half of the skirt at the opposite end* (**Diagram C**).

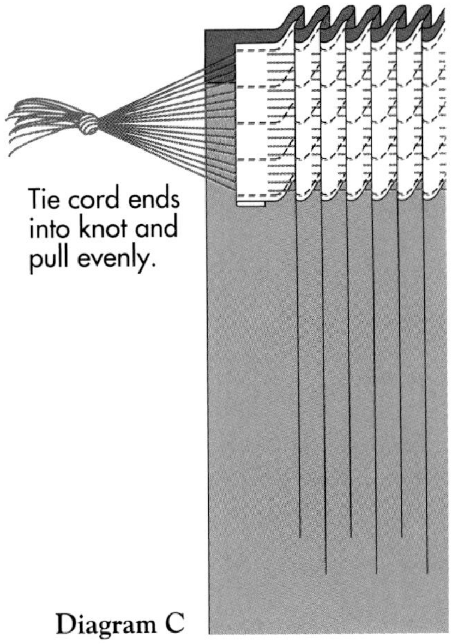

Stitch along blue stitching lines.

Diagram B

Tie cord ends into knot and pull evenly.

Diagram C

Stitch 'n Stretch Elastic

The key to the Express Skirt is **Stitch 'n Stretch Elastic**. It's available in 1½" and 2½" widths and has a woven polyester band with rows of spandex elastic cording threaded through it. The elastic is stitched to the fabric along the blue stitching lines (white stitching lines on black elastic), and then the spandex cords are drawn to fit. You'll find many more uses for this novel elastic.

Stitch 'n Stretch Elastic

Express Skirt (*continued*)

5. Zigzag along each end of the Stitch 'n Stretch in the seam allowance to secure the cords. Trim the cords (**Diagram D**).

6. With right sides together and raw edges aligned, straightstitch the side seam using a ⅝" seam allowance. Press the seam open.

7. Press under the bottom edge 2" and hem, using your favorite method.

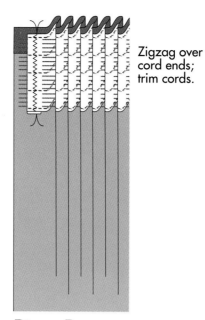

Zigzag over cord ends; trim cords.

Diagram D

Double needle stitching hem

Double (Twin) Needle

Quickly stitch a narrow hem on a knit or woven Express Skirt with a double needle. (This needle works on any zigzag sewing machine that threads from front to back.) A double needle consists of two needles mounted on a single needle shank. It requires two threads on the top of the machine. As the machine stitches, the bobbin thread moves back and forth between the two top threads, producing two lines of straight stitching on the right side of the fabric and a zigzag stitch on the wrong side. Use a size 4.0 or 3.0 double needle for knits.

Darts

A dart is a mainstay in most skirt and pant patterns. Here's how to sew an accurate dart express-style.

1. To prepare the dart:

• Mark the dart "legs" with nips (¼" clips).

• On the wrong side of the fabric, mark the point of the dart with a pin or a fabric marking pencil.

• Fold the dart, right sides together and raw edges aligned, matching the nip markings at the cut edge.

2. To mark the dart with a thread guide:

• Place the fabric under the presser foot and lower the needle into the fabric at the nip marking. Grasp the top thread and pull so that you have a thread tail longer than the dart.

• Lower the presser foot and lay the thread on top of the fabric, angling it toward the point. This thread guide will mark the stitching line between the nips and the dart point (**Diagram A**).

3. To sew the dart:

• Stitch in place several times to lock the stitching.

• Adjust the stitch length to medium and, using the thread as a guide, stitch the dart.

4. To finish the dart point:

• At the end of the dart, turn the machine's wheel by hand, barely catching three to four stitches along the fold.

• Stitch off the fabric 1" to 2", forming a chain of thread (**Diagram B**). Secure the chained thread tail by sewing two or three stitches in place in the dart underlay (**Diagram C**).

• Trim the thread ends.

5. Press the dart flat.

(Continued on page 58)

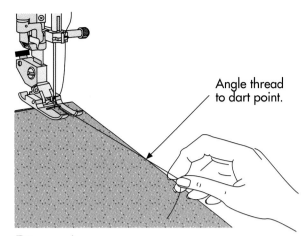

Angle thread to dart point.

Diagram A

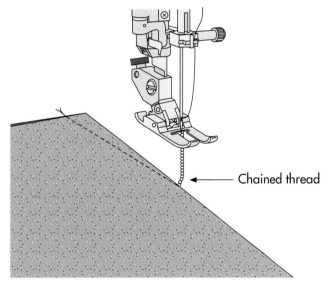

Chained thread

Diagram B

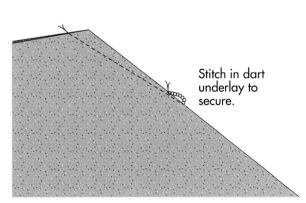

Stitch in dart underlay to secure.

Diagram C

Darts (*continued*)

6. To press the dart over a dress-maker's ham to shape the dart area:

• On lightweight to medium-weight fabrics, press vertical darts toward the center and press horizontal darts downward. Stop pressing ¼" from the dart point.

• On bulky fabrics, cut the dart open, stopping ½" from the dart point. Press the dart flat and then open. To avoid a "dimple" at the dart point, insert a metal darning needle to fill in the dart point and press over the needle (**Diagram D**). Remove the needle.

7. Shape-press the dart from the right side over the dressmaker's ham, using a press cloth to prevent the fabric from becoming shiny.

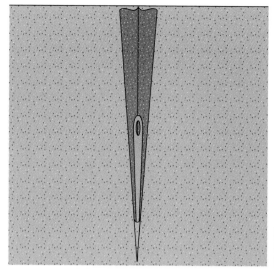

Insert metal darning needle to fill in dart point; press.

Diagram D

Dressmaker's or Tailor's Ham

*A **dressmaker's or tailor's ham** is a must-have tailoring/dressmaking notion. You will use it for pressing darts, sleeves, and curved seams. A ham is covered with a cotton fabric on one side and a wool blend on the other. It is filled with sawdust or a molded material that will not break down with wear. A molded form costs more but will not shift, sag, or attract mildew. The ham holder acts as a "third hand" to keep the ham in place.*

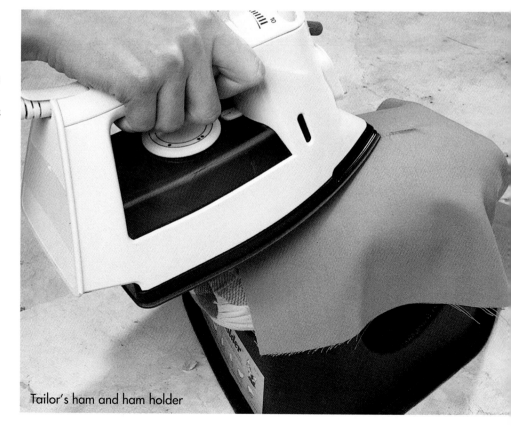

Tailor's ham and ham holder

"Hand-Picked" Zipper in a Flash!

Zippers can offer quite a challenge—especially trying to achieve straight stitching lines. With the hand-picked zipper-by-machine method, you can put all these worries behind you. This technique works best with textured fabrics, such as woolens, tweeds, corduroys, or nubby surfaced fabrics, because the stitches blend well with the fabrics.

1. Cut the skirt pattern with a 1" seam allowance at the center back.

Note from Nancy: I prefer to cut out my skirt patterns with a 1" seam allowance at the center back. The extra width makes it easier to insert the lapped zipper, giving you a greater margin when top-stitching the left side.

2. Stitch the center back seam with a 1" seam allowance. Use a standard stitch length from the hem to the dot and a basting stitch in the zipper area. Press the seam flat and then open.

3. Purchase a zipper at least 1" to 2" longer than you need.

Note from Nancy: I always buy a zipper longer than the opening. I extend the extra length above the zipper opening to eliminate the problem of sewing next to the zipper pull, which often results in crooked stitching.

4. To stitch the right zipper tape:
• Fold the garment fabric so that only the right seam allowance is exposed.
• Open the zipper. With right sides together, place the right zipper tape on the right seam allowance, butting the zipper teeth next to the basted seam. Extend the zipper length above the seam.
• Machine-baste the right zipper tape to the right seam allowance using a zigzag stitch **(Diagram A).**

(Continued on page 60)

Hand-picked zipper

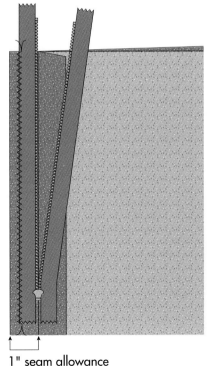

Baste right zipper tape to right seam allowance with zigzag stitch.

1" seam allowance

Diagram A

"Hand-Picked" Zipper *(continued)*

• Attach the zipper foot.

• Set the machine for a straight stitch with a medium-length stitch.

• Close the zipper. Flip the zipper so that the right side faces up. Fold the seam allowance so that a 1/4" fold forms next to the zipper teeth.

• Straightstitch within the fold area, approximately 1/8" from the zipper teeth (**Diagram B**).

5. To stitch left zipper tape:

• Flip the seam allowance over the zipper. Trim the left seam allowance even with the zipper tape (**Diagram C**).

• Fold the left side of the skirt over the zipper.

• Fold back the skirt fabric along the left side of the zipper tape and the seam allowance until 1/4" of the seam allowance is exposed.

• Attach the blindhem foot and set your machine for a blindhem stitch.

> **Note from Nancy:** *Adjust the "zag" of the blindhem stitch according to the thickness and the texture of the fabric test sample. The stitch should just catch the edge of the fold. If the stitch is too wide, it will be visible on the right side of the skirt. If it is too narrow, it will not catch the fold.*

• Starting at the bottom of the zipper, sew with a blindhem stitch, guiding the blindhem foot next to the garment fold. The straight stitches will be in the seam allowances and the zipper tape, and the "zag" of the blindhem stitch will catch the fold (**Diagram D**).

6. Turn the garment to the right side and remove the basting stitches.

7. Open the zipper and bar-tack across the top of the teeth, close to the fabric edge. Cut off the tape above the bar tack (**Diagram E**).

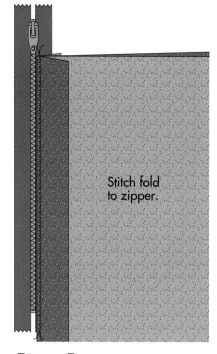

Stitch fold to zipper.

Diagram B

Trim seam allowance even with zipper tape.

Diagram C

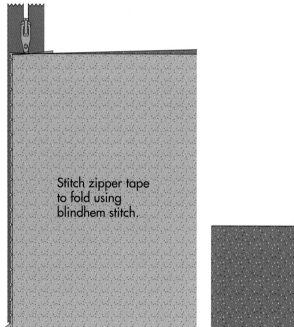

Stitch zipper tape to fold using blindhem stitch.

Diagram D

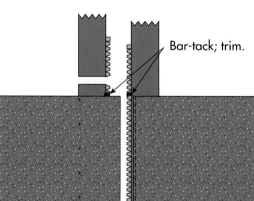

Bar-tack; trim.

Diagram E

Express Lining

This quick-and-easy skirt lining method requires no hand sewing and a minimum of machine sewing. If your skirt has a hemline slit, you will appreciate the timesaving feature of this tulip-shaped lining—a unique curved shape and it won't even peek out!

1. To create a new back lining pattern:

• Place a length of waxed paper over the pattern and, using a marker, trace the waist, side seam, and center back cutting lines. (NOTE: If the center back has a pleat extension, draw a straight cutting line at the center back as illustrated.)

• Mark the hemline ½" shorter than the finished hemline **(Diagram A)**.

• Mark the lower end of the zipper opening with a dot on the center back seam line.

• To make a tulip shape for a skirt with a hemline split:

— Measure and mark 7" up from the corner of the center back at the bottom edge (A). Measure 7" from the center back at the bottom edge (B) and 3" on a diagonal line from the bottom center back (C).

— Connect the dots to form the hemline curve **(Diagram B)**.

• Cut out the back lining using this new pattern.

2. To create a new front lining pattern:

• Place waxed paper over the pattern and trace the waist, the side seam, and the center front.

• Mark the hemline ½" shorter than the finished length.

• Cut out the front lining using this new pattern.

(Continued on page 62)

Express Lining

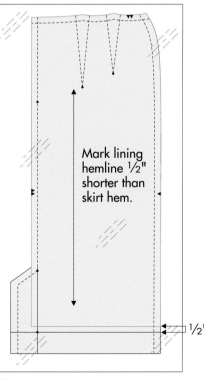

Mark lining hemline ½" shorter than skirt hem.

½"

Diagram A

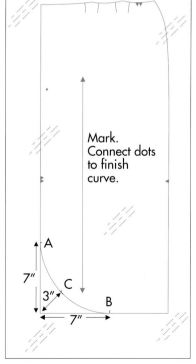

Mark. Connect dots to finish curve.

A

7"

3"

C

B

7"

Diagram B

Express Lining (*continued*)

3. Pin the front and back lining together at the side seams. If the pattern has darts or pleats, mark only the top of the darts or the pleats with nips.

4. Pin the center back seam. Stitch the seam between the top of the hemline curve and the dot for the zipper opening.

• Press under ¾" at the center back zipper opening and gradually taper to the ⅝" stitched seam allowances. Press.

• Clean-finish the raw edges of the seam with a zigzag stitch. Or try using an overcast guide foot and Seams Great or narrow lace, or stitch a rolled hem on a conventional machine or serger (**Diagram D**).

5. To join the lining to the skirt:

• Stitch the skirt side seams and pockets.

• Slip the lining inside the skirt, wrong sides together. Pin the side seams of the skirt and the lining together at the waistline.

• Pin the pressed-under seam allowances of the center back to the zipper area.

6. To form the lining darts and tucks:

• Pin (do not stitch) a tuck in the lining at each waistline dart and/or pleat position. The darts may be deeper than the normal size, since the lining must be smaller in order to fit properly inside the skirt.

• Pin the tucks in the opposite direction of the skirt darts or pleats to eliminate bulk.

Note from Nancy: *Lining darts are not visible from the outside and can easily be formed by tucking instead of sewing. Tucking the lining darts instead of sewing them is definitely an express technique, plus the lining still fits perfectly inside the skirt!*

7. Machine-baste the skirt and the lining together along the waistline (**Diagram E**).

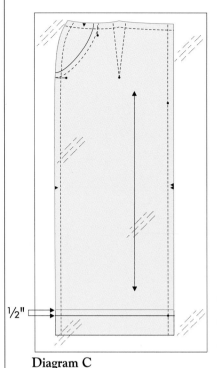

Note from Nancy: *If your pattern has front pockets, pin the skirt and the pocket pattern together with seams overlapping, creating a complete front skirt shape* (**Diagram C**).

½"

Trace.
Mark front lining
hemline ½" shorter
than skirt hem.

Diagram C

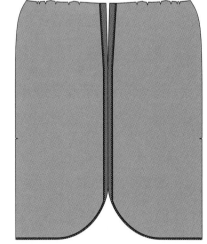

Press under ¾" at
center back opening.
Clean-finish raw
edges.

Diagram D

Form tucks; machine-baste skirt
and lining together at waist.

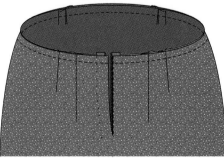

Note from Nancy: *I generally attach the lining to the skirt only at the waistline and let it hang freely at the zipper. One of my staff members chooses to hand-sew the skirt lining to the zipper tape. Either method works!*

Diagram E

Fit & Stretch waistband

Fit & Stretch Waistband

This waistband has the look of a fitted band and the comfort of a stretchable band! The secret is to use elastic instead of interfacing—and to follow these express sewing steps.

1. To cut and prepare the waistband:

• Cut the new waistband pattern 3½" wide and the length of the garment waistline, plus 2" for the seam allowance and underlay extension.

• Clean-finish one lengthwise seam by zigzagging, serging, or using Seams Great.

• Mark the lengthwise fold line, 1⅝" from the clean-finished edge. Fold and press **(Diagram A)**.

2. Insert the zipper.

(Continued on page 64)

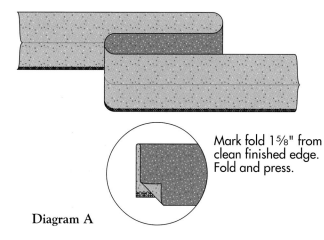

Mark fold 1⅝" from clean finished edge. Fold and press.

Diagram A

Fit & Stretch Waistband *(continued)*

3. To join the waistband to the garment:

• Pin the unfinished edge of the waistband to the garment, right sides together, extending the waistband ⅝" beyond the lapped (left) side of the zipper opening. On the underlay side, the waistband will extend approximately 1½" beyond the zipper opening.

• Stitch the waistband to the waistline using a ⅝" seam **(Diagram B)**.

• Grade the seam allowances and press the waistband and the seam allowances up.

4. To add elastic to the waistline:

• Fold the waistband along the fold line, right sides together.

• Place 1"-wide nonroll elastic on top of the waistband, cutting the elastic slightly longer than the waistband.

• Pin one elastic end at the waistline center back seam, with raw edges even, and stitch the seam, catching the elastic in the seam **(Diagram C)**. Stitch a second time.

• Grade the seam allowance and angle-cut the corner.

• Place a bodkin, a safety pin, or an elastic glide on the free end of the elastic to prevent the elastic from twisting.

• Turn the waistband to the right side, encasing the elastic. The waistband facing will extend about ¼" beyond the stitching line. Press the waistband to the 1¼" finished size.

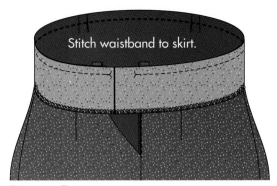

Stitch waistband to skirt.

Diagram B

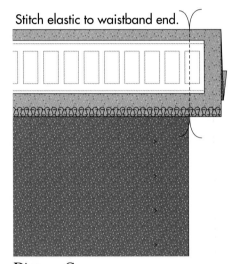

Stitch elastic to waistband end.

Diagram C

Elastic Glide

*The **Elastic Glide** is a great notion to use when inserting elastic in a casing. The flat glide not only guides the elastic through the casing, it also prevents the elastic from twisting.*

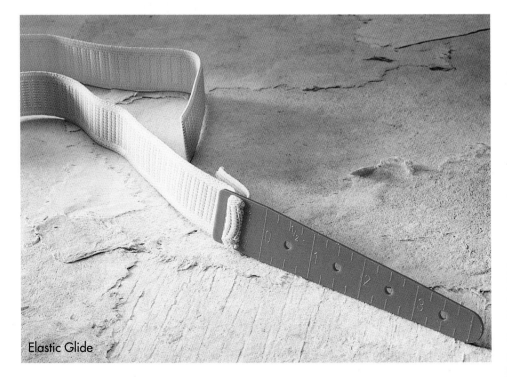

Elastic Glide

5. Work from the garment's right side and stitch in-the-ditch in the waistband seam to attach the underside of the waistband **(Diagram D)**. The elastic is still floating inside the waistband.

Note from Nancy: Stitching in-the-ditch prevents the facing from rolling to the right side. On the right side of the skirt, stitch in the groove (ditch) of the skirt/waistband seam through all layers of the facing and the garment.

6. To fit your garment:
• Try on the garment.
• Pull the elastic to the correct tightness.
• Pin through all the layers at the underlay extension and cut off the excess elastic.

7. To finish the waistband:
• Zigzag or satin-stitch the unfinished end of the waistband, sewing through all the layers, including the elastic.
• Trim any excess elastic or fabric whiskers.
• Stitch a decorative box on both the lapped and underlapped sides of the waistband to keep the elastic flat at the closure **(Diagram E)**.
• Sew on buttons or hooks and eyes as desired.

Note from Nancy: One of the great advantages of this technique is that fabric bulk is eliminated at the waistband end. If you're concerned about the stitches on the underlay, keep in mind that they will be covered when the waistband is lapped together.

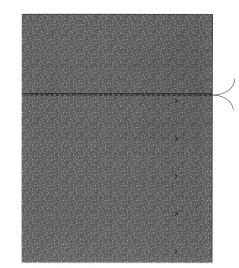

Stitch in-the-ditch.
Diagram D

Stitch decorative box at waistband ends.

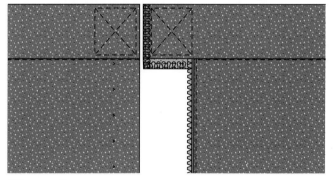

Diagram E

Zip-to-the-Top Waistband

When you're confident of the fit for your skirt size, the Zip-to-the-Top Waistband is the perfect way to increase your sewing speed. Make the waistband plain or express-ive, narrow or wide. The choice is yours. Whatever your decision, the zipper extends to the top of the waistband, eliminating the need for a button or a hook and eye closure!

Skirt zipper closure

1. To modify the waistband pattern:

• For a 1¼"-wide finished waistband, cut the width of the waistband 3½". For a 2"-wide finished waistband, cut the width of the waistband 5". Use the waistband pattern piece to cut the length, with ⅝" seam allowances at the center back.

• Cut out the waistband pattern piece with the unnotched lengthwise edge along the selvage. If you have two raw edges, clean-finish the unnotched edge after applying the interfacing (see Step 2 below).

> **Note from Nancy:** *The unnotched edge will be exposed inside the skirt. If possible, when cutting out the waistband pieces, align the unnotched edge with the selvage of the fabric. Presto! The edge is finished.*

• Place nips in the waistband piece at each notch marking (**Diagram A**).

2. To prepare the waistband:

• Fold the waistband, wrong sides together, allowing the notched edge to extend ⅜" (**Diagram B**).

• Interface the waistband with Waist*Shaper. Fuse the Waist*Shaper to the wrong side of the waistband (**Diagram C**).

• Clean-finish the unnotched edge, if it was not placed along the selvage.

Pellon Waist*Shaper

*Waist*Shaper, a specialty interfacing for waistbands, is available for finished waistband widths of 1¼" and 2". Position the perforations along the waistband fold line and extend the wider side to the unnotched edge of the band. Waist*Shaper is an express-style way to add body to your waistband!*

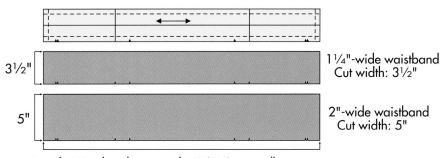

3½" 1¼"-wide waistband
Cut width: 3½"

5" 2"-wide waistband
Cut width: 5"

Length: Waistband pattern plus 2 (⅝") seam allowances

Diagram A

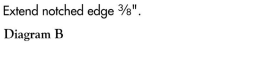

⅜" Extend notched edge ⅜".

Diagram B

Fuse Waist*Shaper to waistband.

Diagram C

Waist*Shaper

Express-ive Channel Stitching

Direct from a designer's workroom: channel stitching! It's especially attractive on the 2"-wide waistband and becomes an express-style accent.

1. Thread the top of the machine with topstitching thread or two threads of the same color. Use a topstitching needle to reduce the chance of skipped stitches.

2. Place the interfacing side of the band toward the feed dogs. Straight-stitch, starting ¼" from the pressed fold, using the edge of the presser foot as a guide. Stitch additional rows ¼" apart on the front side of the waistband **(Diagram A)**.

3. To stitch the waistband to the skirt:

• Stitch the darts or the pleats in the front and back skirt sections.

• Stitch the skirt front to the skirt back at the side seams, leaving the center back seam unstitched **(Diagram B)**.

• Pin the waistband to the skirt, right sides together. Stitch using a ⅝" seam allowance.

• Grade the seam allowances, with the waistband seam allowance narrower than the skirt seam allowance. Press the seam toward the waistband **(Diagram C)**.

4. Stitch the center back seam of the skirt and the waistband. Use a machine basting stitch in the zipper area. Stop stitching at the waistband fold line. Press the seam open **(Diagram D)**.

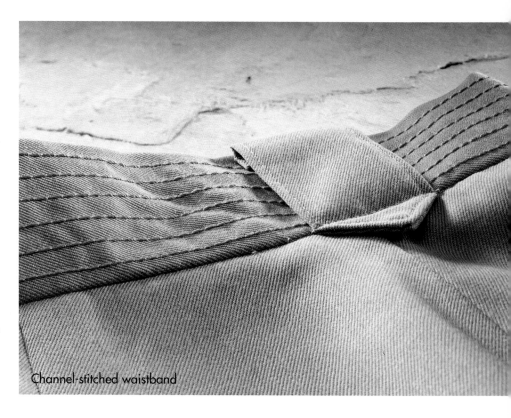

Channel-stitched waistband

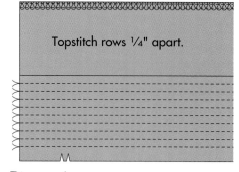

Topstitch rows ¼" apart.

Diagram A

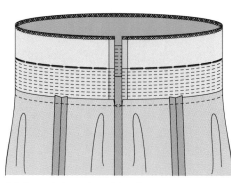

Stitch side seams; leave center back seam unstitched.

Diagram B

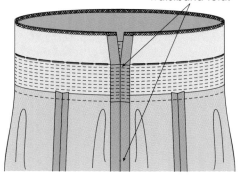

Stitch waistband to skirt. Press seam toward waistband.

Diagram C

Baste opening to waistband fold.

Diagram D

5. To position the zipper:

• Purchase a zipper 2" to 3" longer than the zipper opening to extend the zipper into the waistband.

• Attach a zipper foot to the machine.

• Open the zipper. With right sides together, place the right zipper tape on the right seam allowance, aligning the zipper teeth and the seam.

• Machine-baste the right zipper tape to the right seam allowance. Close the zipper **(Diagram E)**. Flip over the skirt.

6. To topstitch the zipper in place:

• On the right side of the skirt, center Sewer's Fix-it Tape or ½"-wide all-purpose tape over the basted seam so that the tape extends ¼" on either side of the seam. The tape acts as a stitching guide.

• Beginning at the center of the zipper bottom, stitch next to the tape, but not through it, from the bottom to the top. Repeat on the second side of the tape **(Diagram F)**.

• Remove the tape and the basting stitches.

7. To secure the waistband edges:

• Fold under the unstitched edges of the waistband and cover the zipper tape. Handstitch the band to the zipper.

• Working from the right side, pin the lengthwise waistband edge in place.

• Stitch in-the-ditch from the right side along the lower waistband edge, securing the unsewn waistband facing seam allowance **(Diagram G)**.

Sewer's Fix-it Tape

I prefer using ½"-wide Sewer's Fix-it Tape as a stitching guide. It is softer than household tape and can be repositioned several times without losing its stickiness.

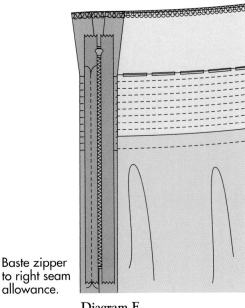

Baste zipper to right seam allowance.

Diagram E

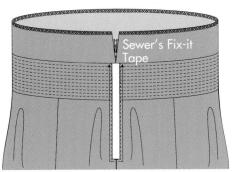

Topstitch from bottom to top on right side.

Diagram F

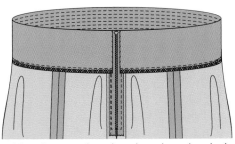

Fold under waistband and stitch in-the-ditch.

Diagram G

Sewer's Fix-it Tape

Express-ive Tabs

If you like the look and the fit of a belted skirt or pants, here's a fast, designer accent. It looks great on the channel-stitched waistband, page 68.

1. Cut a 15" x 3½" strip of fabric. Cut a strip of lightweight interfacing the same size.

> **Note from Nancy:** *I do not usually include the interfacing in the entire seam allowance. But since these are only ¼" seams, it's faster to fuse the entire piece, and the bulk in the seams is minimal.*

2. Fuse lightweight interfacing to the wrong side of the fabric **(Diagram A)**.

3. To stitch the tabs:
• Adjust your sewing machine to a short stitch length.
• With right sides together, align the long edges and stitch using a ¼" seam.
• Press the seam open and offset the seam so that it is slightly to the right or the left of center to reduce bulk **(Diagram B)**.
• Cut the tube into four 3¾"-long sections.

4. To create each tab:
• Measure and mark the center point of one of the unstitched tab ends.
• Place the tip of a ruler, or any square corner, on the center and mark the cutting lines for the tab point at a 45° angle **(Diagram C)**.
• Cut along the marked lines to form the tab point. Stitch the point using a ¼" seam and grade the seam. Turn the tab right side out, press, and edgestitch. Use a Collar Point & Tube Turner (see page 17) for easy turning **(Diagram D)**.

Skirt tab

Fuse interfacing to fabric.

Diagram A

Stitch tube.
Offset seam.

Diagram B

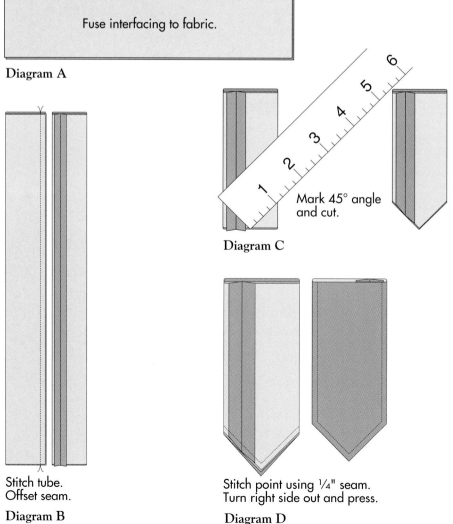

Mark 45° angle and cut.

Diagram C

Stitch point using ¼" seam.
Turn right side out and press.

Diagram D

5. To position the tabs on the finished waistband:

• Measure and mark 2½" to 3" (the larger measurement is for larger waist measurements) on each side of the side seams.

• Place the side edges of one of the tabs at each mark and extend the points below the waistband lower edge. Pin in place (**Diagram E**).

• Fold under the raw edge of each tab so that the fold is even with the top edge of the waistband. Press the fold.

• Try on the waistband to check for tab placement and fit. Two tabs should be on the band front and two on the back.

6. To join the tabs to the waistband:

• Remove the pins and flip tabs up.

• On the right side of the waistband, stitch ⅛" from the top edge to secure the tabs. Trim the tab seams to ¼" (**Diagram F**).

• Flip the tabs down and pin them to the waistband. Stitch in-the-ditch from the right side along the lower waistband edge, securing the tabs (**Diagram G**).

7. Add optional buttons at the lower edge of the front tabs.

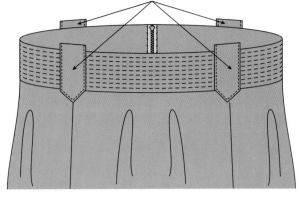

Position tabs on right side of waistband.

Diagram E

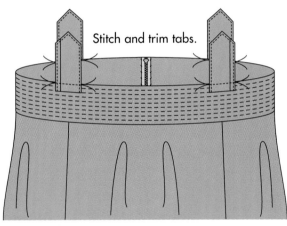

Stitch and trim tabs.

Diagram F

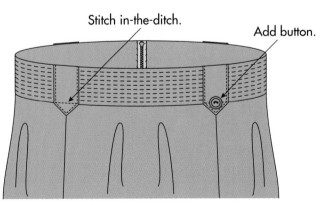

Stitch in-the-ditch.

Add button.

Diagram G

Pants—Express Style!

The sewing techniques for pants follow the same streamlined concepts as for skirts, jackets, and blouses. Yet the process can be even more timesaving if two or more pairs of pants are made at once. I guarantee that it takes only a little more time to sew and, when you are finished, you have two pairs of pants instead of one.

Express Pants

Crisp Creases

Before sewing one stitch on my pants, I like to establish the front crease. Here are two options; both are fast yet leave a lasting "impression"! And while the front creases are drying, a second pair can be pressed.

Pressing creases:

1. Establish the front crease by folding each pant front with the wrong sides together and matching the cut edges at the hem and the crotch. The edges between the crotch and the hem may not meet due to the shaping of the leg—do not force the edges to meet (**Diagram A**).

2. Place a press cloth on the fold and press between the crotch and the hem with a steam iron. Lift the iron and set the crease with a Tailor Clapper.

3. Let the pant front dry five to 10 minutes to assure a sharp crease.

4. The back crease will be pressed after the legs are sewn together.

(Continued on page 74)

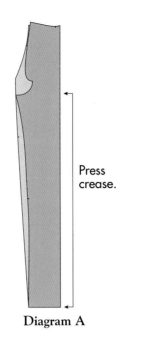

Press crease.

Diagram A

Tailor Clapper
The Tailor Clapper is a 9" x 2½" hardwood block especially designed to flatten and crease. After pressing a crease with a steam iron, place the wooden block on the crease and hold it in place for five seconds. The moisture from the fabric is absorbed into the wood and sets the crease. Do not "pound" the crease; simply holding the block in place is the best technique.

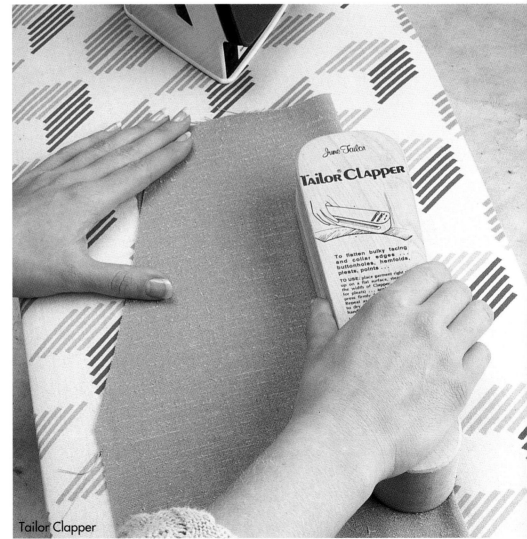

Tailor Clapper

Crisp Creases (*continued*)

Fusing creases:

This crease idea comes from a viewer of "Sewing With Nancy," Rosann Hutchins from Redlands, California. Her thought is to use ThreadFuse (see page 33) in the bobbin and Wash-A-Way Basting Thread in the top. The results are phenomenal!

1. Wind ThreadFuse in the bobbin and thread Wash-A-Way Basting Thread in the top of the machine.

2. Establish pressed creases as explained in Step 1 of "Pressing creases," page 73. Slightly press the crease between the hem and the crotch.

3. Open the front crease and stitch from the right side along the crease mark. Refold the crease and press with a damp press cloth. The ThreadFuse will create a permanent crease and the basting thread will disappear when pressed with a damp cloth (**Diagram B**).

Stitch along crease mark.

Diagram B

> **Note from Nancy:** *When I am constructing a pair of pants, I like to prepress the hem after I've fused or pressed the creases. See "Express Hems," page 82.*

Wash-A-Way Basting Thread

This savvy thread dissolves in water or with the heat of an iron and a damp press cloth! It's a great idea to store this thread, on the spool and on a bobbin, in a clearly marked package to indicate that it washes away.

Wash-A-Way Basting Thread

Seaming Sequence

Combine this express-style seaming sequence with the finger pinning technique that follows to achieve a professional look in a short amount of time.

1. To stitch the side seam:

• With right sides together, align the front and back legs at the side seam.

• Stitch the side seam from hem to waistline (**Diagram A**).

2. Press the seam flat. Press the seam open over a sleeve roll or use a Seam Stick to prevent the seam edges from leaving an imprint on the right side. (See Seam Stick, page 41.)

3. To stitch the inseam:

• Match the cut edges of the inseam from the pant hem to the knee. (This is the halfway point of the inseam.)

> *Note from Nancy: In a quality pant pattern, the back inseam will be ½" shorter than the front inseam to give you a smoother fit in the thigh. To make the seams' edges meet, sew with the longer layer (the front) against the feed dogs. The job of the feed dogs is to "bite" or ease the lower layer as the presser foot, with its smooth bottom surface, pushes the top layer. These two counter movements cause uneven lengths of fabric to meet. When using this easing technique, the other pant leg must be sewn with the greatest amount of fabric to the right of the needle. It may seem awkward at first, but the smooth results are worth the effort!*

• Stitch the inseam from the hem to the knee.

• At the knee, stretch the back inseam to meet the front inseam and continue to sew the remaining half of the inseam (**Diagram B**).

4. Press the inseam open using a sleeve roll. Turn the legs right side out.

5. To set the back crease:

• Fold the pants along the front crease. Anchor this crease with a sleeve board or other sewing/pressing tool to prevent the pants from shifting while you press.

• Press the back crease from the hem toward the crotch. The fabric will naturally fold, forming an "inch pinch" near the crotch area (**Diagram C**).

• Use a Tailor Clapper (see page 73) to set the crease. Allow the pants to dry.

> *Note from Nancy: You'll probably never find the term "inch pinch" in another sewing book, yet it accurately depicts what automatically happens in the back inner thigh area.*

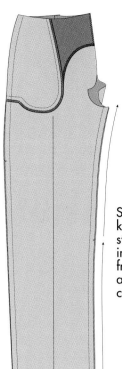

Stitch outer seam.
Diagram A

Stitch inseam to knee. Then stretch back inseam to meet front inseam and stitch to crotch.

Diagram B

Inch pinch

Diagram C

Finger Pinning

Try "finger pinning" when sewing long, straight seams. A perfect time to try this express sewing method is when sewing the inner and outer seams of pants. After stitching a seam or two using the finger pinning method, you'll be convinced that all long seams can be sewn express-style.

1. Place the fabric under the presser foot and lock the stitches, sewing two or three stitches with the stitch length set at "0."

2. Match the raw edges at the top end of the seam; hold the fabric together with your right hand and pull the fabric taut.

3. At the middle of the seam, pinch the raw edges together with your left hand. Transfer the fabric to your right hand without letting go of the end you have already pinched.

4. From the middle of the seam to the bottom (which is under the presser foot), match raw edges and pinch together at 6" to 8" intervals, always transferring the fabric to your right hand. Now you have four to five pleats or "finger pins" of fabric in your right hand (see photograph).

• Use your left fingers to hold the fabric layers together by placing your fingers parallel to the seam, as if you were playing the flute.

• Sew to the first fabric pleat. Release a pleat and continue to sew. When you reach the second half of the seam, finger-pin again.

Finger pinning

Note from Nancy: *Finger pinning is not just for pants. Also use this speed-sewing technique when stitching side seams of skirts, dresses and tops. I use this technique on practically all side seams, except when the fabric is a plaid!*

Pocket Extension

Try this side pocket extension on your next pair of pants. You'll really notice a difference in the way your pants fit. The extension prevents the pocket from pulling out of shape or creating a bulge at the pleats or the tucks.

1. To extend the pocket facing pattern:

• Fold the darts or the pleats on the pant front pattern.

• Position the pocket facing pattern on top of the pant front pattern, matching the pocket seams to the pant seams. Pin or tape waxed paper or tissue paper on the facing pattern, extending the extra paper to the center front.

• Trace the extended waistline and 4" down the center cut edge (**Diagram A**).

• Extend the lower edge of the extension to meet the pocket facing.

2. Cut out the new pocket facing pattern from the lining fabric (**Diagram B**).

3. Use the original pocket pattern and cut out the pocket from the fashion fabric.

4. With right sides together and raw edges aligned, pin the facing to the pant front. Stitch the pocket facing to the slanted edge of the pant front and press. Grade the seam allowances with the pocket facing seam allowance narrower than the pant front seam allowance (**Diagram C**).

5. Understitch, sewing the seam allowance to the facing with a multizigzag stitch to prevent the facing from rolling to the outside.

6. To join the pocket to the facing:

• Clean-finish the raw edges of the pocket piece.

• With right sides together and raw edges aligned, pin the pocket to the facing, matching curves.

• Turn right side up and check the alignment of the pocket edge to the circle on the pocket. Match the circles at the lower edge of the pocket.

• Stitch, following the curve of the pocket (**Diagram D**).

7. Fold the pocket facing to the wrong side of the pants and zigzag the pocket facing extension to the pants at the center front (**Diagram E**).

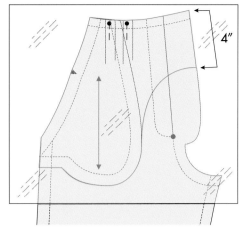

Trace; measure down 4" to extend pocket facing.

Diagram A

Pocket facing

Side pocket

Diagram B

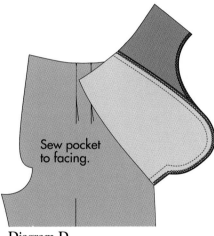

Understitch pocket facing to pants.

Diagram C

Sew pocket to facing.

Diagram D

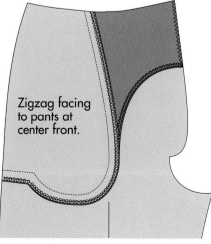

Zigzag facing to pants at center front.

Diagram E

Speedy Two-Seam Fly-Front Zipper

This fly-front zipper application only requires two rows of stitching! You'll wonder why you ever let zippers create stress in your life.

1. For a standard 8" zipper opening, purchase a 9" zipper. Check the pattern to be sure the extension is 1½" from the center front and measures 9" long. If necessary, add width to the extension so that it totals 1½" **(Diagram A)**.

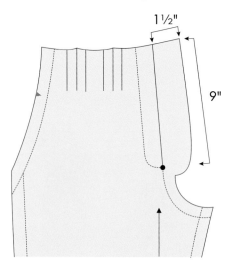

Diagram A

2. To mark the zipper position on the pant fronts:
- Mark the center front of the fabric with a nip.
- On the wrong side, mark the zipper stopping point.
- Mark the pant fronts with *R* and *L* (right and left, as you would wear them) in the waist seam allowance using a washable marking pen.

Two-Seam Fly-Front Zipper

3. To stitch the crotch:

• After the inseam and the side seam are stitched, turn one pant leg right side out and insert it inside the other leg.

• Align the notches, the seams, and the raw edges; pin. Stitch the crotch from the waist edge to the zipper stopping point (**Diagram B**).

• Restitch the crotch seam between the notches and trim the seam to ³⁄₈".

4. To press the crotch extension:

• On the left front, press under ³⁄₄" of the extension so that the fabric cut edge meets the nip.

• On the right front, press under the entire 1¹⁄₂" extension (**Diagram C**).

5. To insert the left side of the zipper:

• Attach a zipper foot and adjust your sewing machine for a straight stitch.

• Place the zipper under the left front extension.

• Position the bottom zipper staple ¹⁄₄" below the zipper opening, with the zipper length extending above the waistline.

• Pin the fabric fold of the left extension ¹⁄₈" from the zipper teeth. Stitch next to the fold (**Diagram D**).

(Continued on page 80)

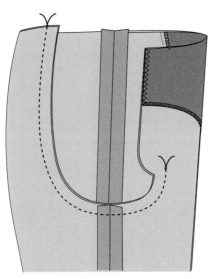

Stitch crotch seam to zipper stopping point.

Diagram B

Diagram C

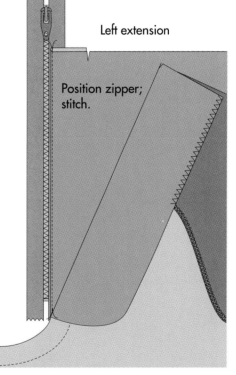

Diagram D

Two-Seam Fly-Front Zipper *(continued)*

6. To stitch the overlap section of the zipper:

• Lap the right front extension over the left, meeting at the center front nips. Pin or tape in place **(Diagram E)**.

• Mark the stitching line using a washable marking pen.

• Topstitch, starting at the bottom of the zipper opening and curving the stitching line to approximately 1" from the fold **(Diagram F)**.

• Remove the tape.

7. Open the zipper and bar-tack across the teeth, close to the fabric cut edge. It's only necessary to bar-tack on one side of the zipper teeth. Trim the tape ¼" above the bar tack **(Diagram G)**.

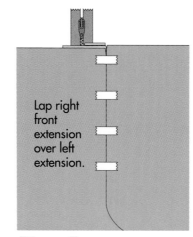

Lap right front extension over left extension.

Diagram E

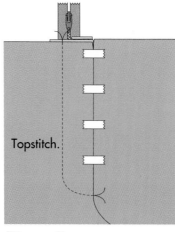

Topstitch.

Diagram F

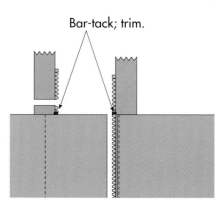

Bar-tack; trim.

Diagram G

Sewer's Fix-it Tape

*I prefer to tape the extension using **Sewer's Fix-it Tape** (Diagram E). Sometimes pinning creates a "dimple," and the resulting stitching is not as straight and smooth as when the extension is taped. After the zipper is completed, the Sewer's Fix-it Tape can be easily removed.*

Fly-Front Zipper Guide

*To save time and ensure accuracy, I use a **Fly-Front Zipper Guide** when topstitching. The guide has tiny plastic "teeth" on its underside. Position the teeth in the seam line so that the distance from the seam line to the edge of the guide is 1". The teeth stabilize the template and hold the guide in place for accurate stitching.*

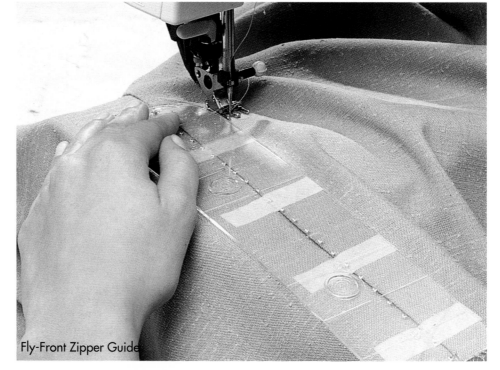

Fly-Front Zipper Guide

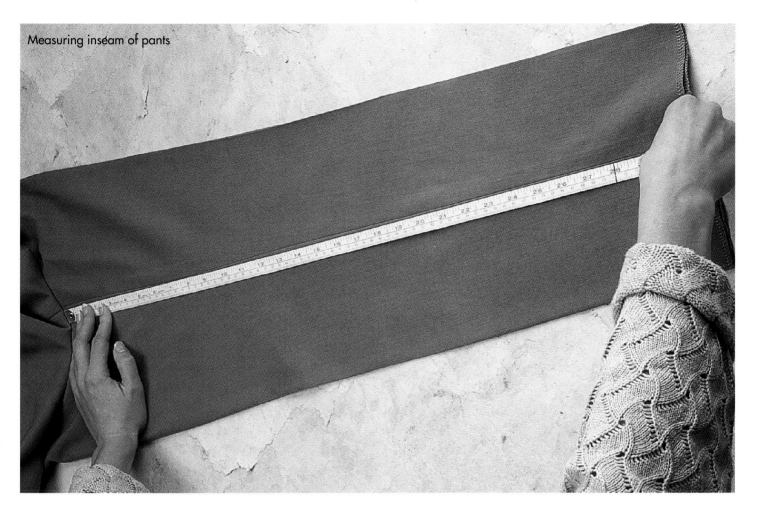

Measuring inseam of pants

Hemming Hints

Prepressing hems while the fabric lies flat makes the final hemming steps a snap! This is a great timesaving technique whether you are sewing children's sleeves, pant hems, or any area that is difficult to press after it is sewn in a circle.

To mark your tape for fast pant measuring:

1. Try on the pants (or a pair of pants that fits you) and place a pin at the desired length.

2. Lay the pants on the ironing board with the creases folded and the inseam and the side seams aligned.

3. Lift one leg and measure the inseam from the crotch to the pin and mark this measurement on your tape measure.

Note from Nancy: By marking the inseam measurement on your tape measure, you will never have to try on pants when hemming (unless you change your mind about length or your size changes). Use your marked tape every time.

Express Hems

Fusing a hem is a fast and easy way to finish the hem. The fusing technique works best on knits and lightweight wovens. Make a quick test sample by fusing the fusible web on a fabric scrap to see if this is the hem finish you would like. For other hemming techniques, see *10-20-30 Minutes To Sew* and *The Best Of Sewing With Nancy*.

Hemming with unbacked fusible web:

1. Place a ½"- to ¾"-wide strip of fusible web along the wrong side of the hem edge.

2. Serge or zigzag the fusible web to the wrong side of the hem edge. Trim any web that extends past the edge **(Diagram A)**.

3. Fold under the hem so that the entire hem is the same width.

4. Cover the hem with a damp press cloth. Press with a steam iron to fuse the hem to the garment **(Diagram B)**.

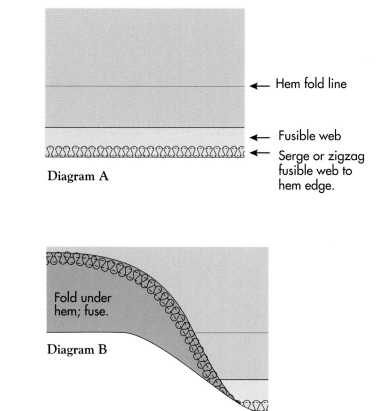

← Hem fold line

← Fusible web

← Serge or zigzag fusible web to hem edge.

Diagram A

Fold under hem; fuse.

Diagram B

Stitch Witchery

Stitch Witchery, an unbacked fusible web, works like a charm for hemming garments. Stitching the fusible web to the hem finishes the edges all in one step. It also keeps the web in place while hemming. When heat is applied, the hem is fused precisely without exposing the web to the iron.

Stitch Witchery

Hemming with paper-backed fusible web:

1. Finish the raw edge by serging or zigzagging.

2. Cut ½"- to ¾"-wide strips of paper-backed fusible web.

3. Position the web side of the paper-backed web to the wrong side of the hem. Place the web ¼" below the hem edge and press.

4. Remove the paper backing (Diagram C).

5. Fold under the hem so that the entire hem is the same width. Fuse (Diagram D).

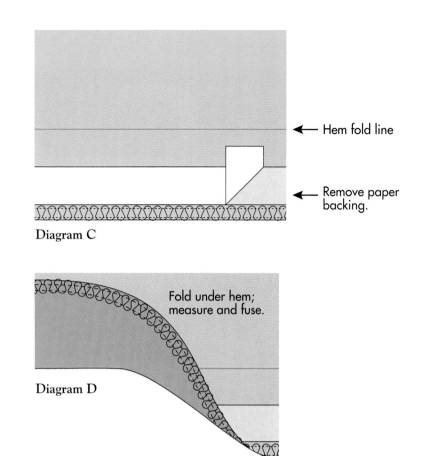

← Hem fold line

← Remove paper backing.

Diagram C

Fold under hem; measure and fuse.

Diagram D

Wonder-Under

Wonder-Under is a paper-backed fusible web. Use narrow strips of Wonder-Under as an express notion to position pockets and fuse hemlines. It is machine washable and dry cleanable.

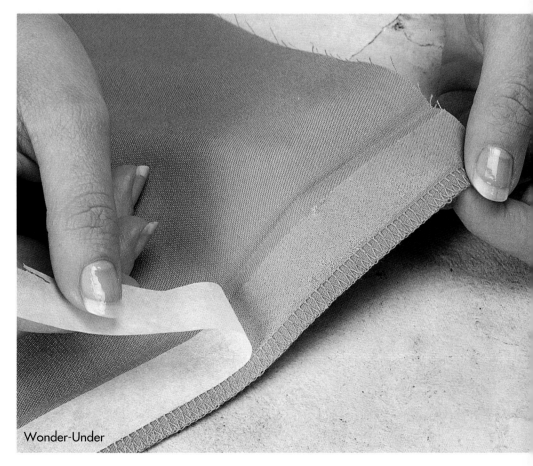

Wonder-Under

Reversibles

Reversibles are the ultimate in sewing express-style. Sew any two or more of these reversibles—jacket, skirt, top, or city shorts—and double your wardrobe options without doubling your sewing time. Since there are only two or three pattern pieces and no facings, linings, or hems, these reversibles stitch up quickly.

Sewing Reversibles

Choosing Fabric

Select two lightweight woven fabrics of comparable weight and width with the same fiber content. Choose two solid colors or a solid and a coordinating print. Fabric choice for reversibles is crucial! If the fabrics are too heavy, the completed garment will not hang properly and will be too stiff. If you're in doubt whether the fabrics are suitable, place two layers together and drape them over your hand. This will give you an idea of the weight of the completed garment.

Note from Nancy: Throughout the instructions, I will refer to the two sides of the reversible garment as the outer and the inner. Either side can be an outer garment, and vice versa, but for construction purposes, choose one side as the outer and the other as the inner!

Selecting the Pattern

Jacket: Choose a classic-style jacket pattern without a collar. The only pattern pieces you need are the jacket front, the jacket back, and the sleeve. Pockets are optional.

Top: Choose a classic-style pull-on top without a collar, ribbing, or set-in sleeves.

Skirt: Use a basic straight skirt pattern with front and back pattern pieces and an elasticized waist.

City Shorts: Choose a basic shorts pattern with an elasticized waist. Use only the front and back shorts pattern pieces.

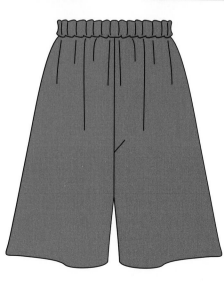

Choose basic/classic styles.

The "Cutting Double" Technique

When making a reversible garment, it is crucial that the inner and outer garments be exactly the same size. An easy way to effectively assure that they're identical is to cut out both at the same time with this simple "cutting double" approach.

1. Place blank newsprint or pattern paper that is slightly larger than the fabric on the cutting surface. Because you will cut through the paper, it prevents the tip of the scissors from catching one layer of the fabric and causing a dimple.

2. Fold each piece of fabric in half, aligning selvage edges.

3. Place one fabric on the paper, aligning the fold with one edge of the paper, and pin. If one fabric is wider than the other, place the wider fabric first.

4. Place the second fabric on top of the other, again aligning the fold with the same edge of the paper. Pin through all layers, making certain the folds of the fabrics are perfectly matched **(Diagram A)**.

5. Position the front and back pattern pieces (plus the sleeve piece, if sewing a jacket) on the fabric **(Diagram B)**. Remember, facings aren't needed.

6. Pin each pattern piece on the grain line, pinning through all layers including the paper. Use pattern weights, such as Weight Mates or Shape Weights, to secure the remaining edges.

7. Cut through all layers, including the paper.

__Note from Nancy:__ This minimal paper cutting will not dull shears. The method makes it easier to cut identical layers since both fabrics are handled as one. Plus, the fabric will not shift, and the scissors can't snag the bottom fabric layer. This paper technique isn't just for cutting double; use this approach with silks and other silk-like fabrics that easily shift during cutting.

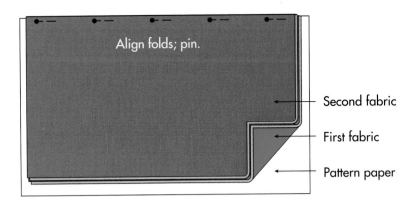

Align folds; pin.

Second fabric

First fabric

Pattern paper

Diagram A

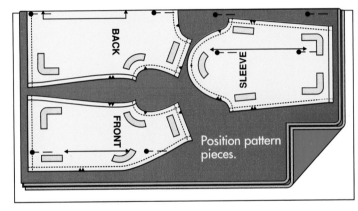

BACK

SLEEVE

FRONT

Position pattern pieces.

Diagram B

Weight Mates or Shape Weights

Pattern weights are essential to express-style sewing and are an efficient method of "pinning" the pattern to the fabric. I usually pin each pattern to the fabric following the grain line of the fabric. Then I place the weights an inch or so from the cutting line on one of the patterns. You need only one set of weights, since you cut only one piece at a time. After cutting out one piece, move the weights to the next piece.

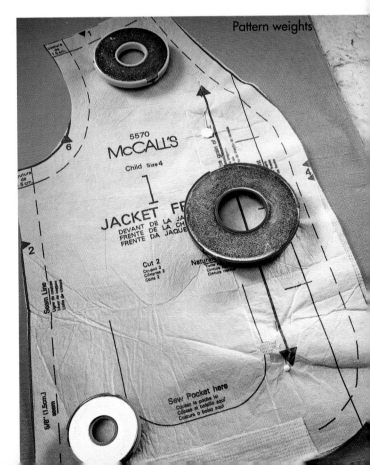

Pattern weights

Reversible Jacket

This reversible jacket is sewn almost entirely by machine with a minimum of sewing. The trick to making this two-way jacket is to follow the unique construction sequence to the letter!

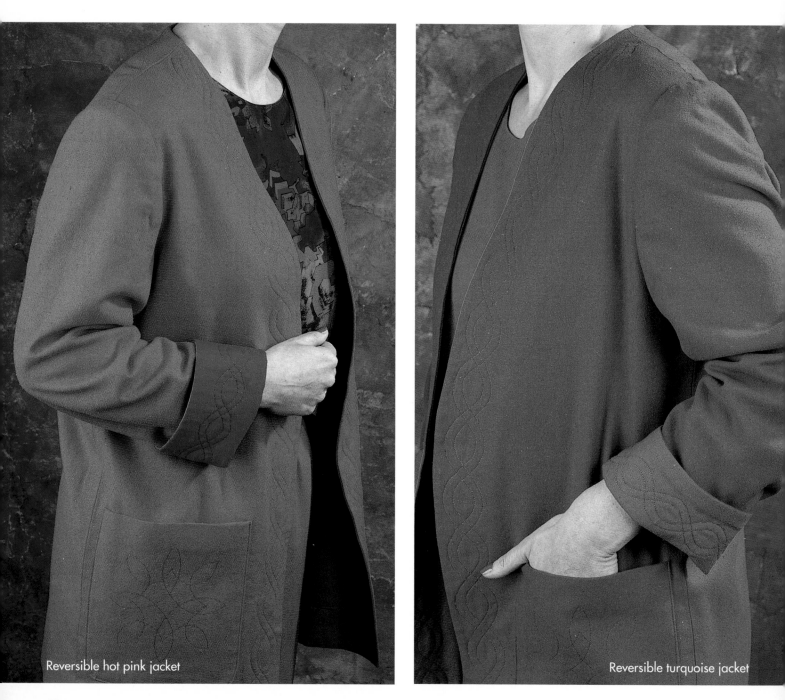

Reversible hot pink jacket

Reversible turquoise jacket

Sewing the Inner and Outer Jackets

1. Trim the hem allowances on the sleeve and jacket pattern pieces to ⅝". These areas will be automatically hemmed when the two layers are stitched together, requiring only a ⅝" seam allowance (**Diagram A**).

2. To create interfacing pattern pieces:

• Working on a padded surface, place waxed paper over the center front of the jacket front pattern.

• Set a 6" hem gauge with a sliding guide at 1". Guide the end of the point of the seam gauge around the cutting line of the pattern at the center front. The gauge will scratch off two lines on the waxed paper, indicating the cutting lines for the interfacing (**Diagram B**).

• Use this same hem gauge technique to make the back interfacing pattern 1" wide.

• Cut out the interfacing pieces.

• Position the interfacing pieces on the wrong side of the outer jacket pieces, placing them ¼" from the outer edges. Fuse in place. The inner jacket does not need interfacing (**Diagram C**).

• Optional: Apply interfacing to the pockets if you are using pockets. Refer to the Lined Patch Pocket, page 34.

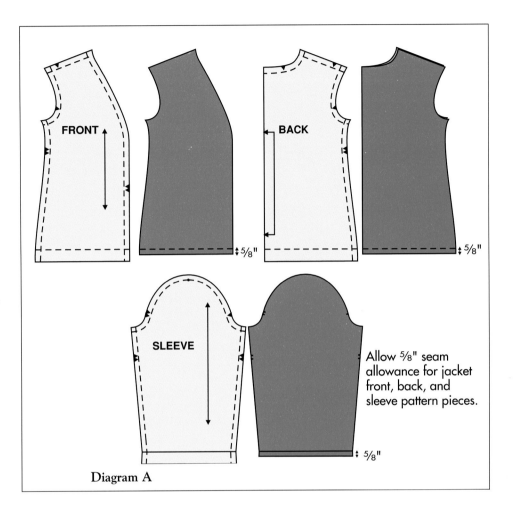

FRONT

BACK

SLEEVE

Allow ⅝" seam allowance for jacket front, back, and sleeve pattern pieces.

↕ ⅝"

Diagram A

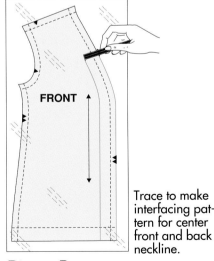

FRONT

Trace to make interfacing pattern for center front and back neckline.

Diagram B

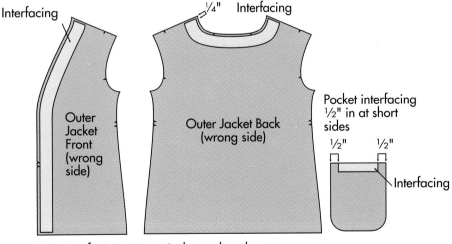

Interfacing

¼"   Interfacing

Outer Jacket Front (wrong side)

Outer Jacket Back (wrong side)

Pocket interfacing ½" in at short sides

½"   ½"

Interfacing

Fuse interfacing to outer jacket and pocket.

Diagram C

(Continued on page 90)

Sewing the Jackets (*continued*)

3. Stitch the shoulder seams of both the outer and inner jackets, creating two separate jackets (**Diagram D**). Press the seams flat and then open.

4. Stitch pockets on the jacket.

5. To set the sleeves in the outer and inner jacket:

• Ease in the sleeve fullness of each sleeve, using one of the easing techniques given on page 24.

Note from Nancy: It is easier to insert a sleeve while both the sleeve and the jacket are still flat. Anytime I can avoid sewing "in circles," I do!

• With right sides together, pin each sleeve to the corresponding armhole opening before stitching underarm seams.

• Stitch each sleeve in place.

• Restitch each underarm by stitching just inside the first row. Trim the seam allowances in the underarm area. Press the seam allowances toward the sleeves (**Diagram E**).

6. To join the side/underarm seam of the outer jacket:

• With right sides together and raw edges aligned, match the sides/underarm seam, the armhole seams, and the notches of the outer jacket. Stitch.

• Reinforce the underarm curve by stitching inside the first stitching line.

• Press the seam flat and then open with a Seam Stick or seam roll (see page 41).

7. To join the side/underarm seam of the inner jacket:

• With right sides together and raw edges aligned, match the sides, the underarm seams, and the notches of the inner jacket (**Diagram F**).

• Stitch the side seams, leaving an 8" opening in one of the side seams for turning. This opening, which will be used to turn the two jackets right side out, is the only area that eventually must be stitched by hand.

• Press the seams flat and then open.

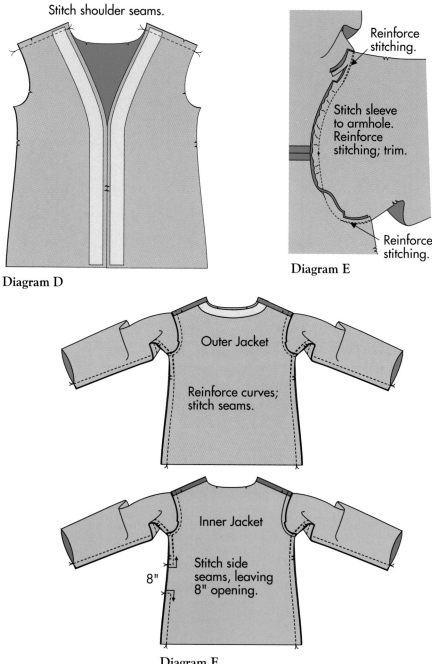

Stitch shoulder seams.

Diagram D

Reinforce stitching.

Stitch sleeve to armhole. Reinforce stitching; trim.

Reinforce stitching.

Diagram E

Outer Jacket

Reinforce curves; stitch seams.

Inner Jacket

Stitch side seams, leaving 8" opening.

8"

Diagram F

Note from Nancy: When leaving an opening in a seam for turning fabric right side out (in this case, the jacket), stitch to the opening, pivot, and stitch to the raw edge. Repeat on the other side of the opening. This reinforces the opening, allows the seam to be more stable, and minimizes raveling. Use this hint on the reversible jacket and any other project in which you leave an opening (**Diagram G**).

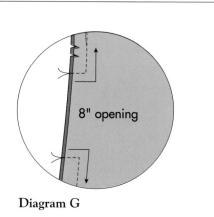

8" opening

Diagram G

Joining the Inner and Outer Jackets

Turning the jackets to the outside will be like pulling a rabbit out of a hat. To accomplish this magic trick, you must follow these steps exactly.

1. To pin the outer and inner jackets together:

• With right sides together and raw edges aligned, match the notches and the seams.

• Trim the shoulder seams on one of the jackets to reduce bulk.

2. To stitch the jackets together along the neckline and the front edges:

• Begin at the hem and stitch the front and neckline edges **(Diagram A)**.

• Trim and grade the seam allowances.

• Press the seam flat and then open.

• Turn the jacket right side out so that the outer jacket is on the outside.

3. To stitch the sleeve hems:

• Turn under ⅝" and finger-press on the lower edge of each inner and outer sleeve. Stack the seams and pin the turned-under edges together at the underarm seams **(Diagram B)**. This aligns the sleeves and prevents twisting after turning wrong side out.

• Insert your hand through the opening in the lower edge of the jacket. Pull the pinned edges of one sleeve to the outside.

• Remove the pin and repin the entire lower edge of the sleeve, right sides together, matching the pressed seam lines. Stitch the hemline edges together in a circle **(Diagram C)**.

• Grade the seam allowances; press the seam flat and then open.

• Insert the sleeve back through the opening.

• Repeat for the other sleeve.

(Continued on page 92)

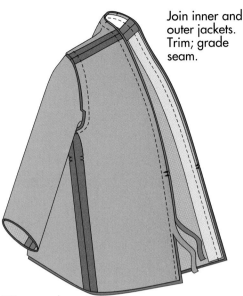

Join inner and outer jackets. Trim; grade seam.

Diagram A

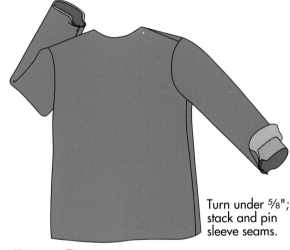

Turn under ⅝"; stack and pin sleeve seams.

Diagram B

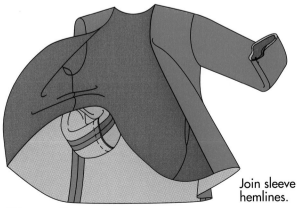

Join sleeve hemlines.

Diagram C

Joining the Jackets (*continued*)

4. To hem the lower edge of the jacket:

• With right sides together, align the hemlines. (Most of the fabric will be tucked inside the jacket.) Pin the edges, making sure the tucked fabric is away from the hem.

• At the outer edges, "wrap" the seam allowances toward the center front so that the stitching line is at the fold. Pin.

> **Note from Nancy:** *Wrapping corners is not just for collars and lapels. Anytime there is a corner, the seam allowances can be wrapped to one side, making it easier to get a sharp, crisp corner.*

• Stitch from one wrapped corner and continue to the opposite corner (**Diagram D**).

• Grade the seam allowances, insert a seam roll or a Seam Stick (see Lined Sleeves—Express Style, page 40) through the side opening, align the seam over the Seam Stick or seam roll, and press.

5. To turn the jacket right side out:

• Insert your hand through the opening and pull the hemmed edges to the outside (**Diagram E**).

• Handstitch the opening closed (**Diagram F**).

6. To add the finishing details:

• Thread the machine with matching threads for the respective jackets, using one color in the top and the other in the bobbin.

• Pin the jackets together at the underarm and shoulder seams.

• Stitch in-the-ditch 1" on each side of the underarm seam to keep the sleeves in place (**Diagram G**).

• Handstitch along the shoulder seam, attaching the two jackets.

• Roll the finished edges between your fingers to center the seam. Pin and press.

• Edgestitch with either matching thread or Wonder Thread around the neck, the front, the lower edges, and the sleeves, starting and stopping at the seam (**Diagram H**).

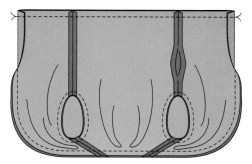

Align hemlines with most of fabric tucked inside jacket; pin. Wrap corners; stitch.

Diagram D

Turn jacket right side out through 8" side opening.

Diagram E

Slipstitch opening closed.

Diagram F

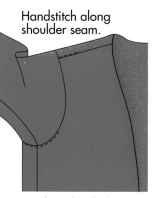

Handstitch along shoulder seam.

Stitch in-the-ditch 1" on each side of underarm seam.

Diagram G

Edgestitch neck, front, lower edges, and sleeves.

Diagram H

Wonder Thread

I like to use **Wonder Thread**—*a clear, nylon, monofilament thread for edgestitching—since it blends with the fabric. It is a light-weight (size 80) thread suit-able for either a serger or a conventional machine and is available in clear or smoke. When pressing a seam stitched with* **Wonder Thread**, *use a press cloth.*

Express-ive Quilting Stitches

A quilted border is a quick yet expressive option that adds a decorative accent to a reversible jacket. An added benefit is that it keeps all the fabric layers together.

Quilting stitches

Quilting the jacket border:

1. Baste and press the jacket edges.

2. Pin a quilting pattern that has been transferred to paper along the front edge of the jacket. Clip through the paper stencils periodically to make them easier to shape around the curved areas **(Diagram A).**

(Continued on page 94)

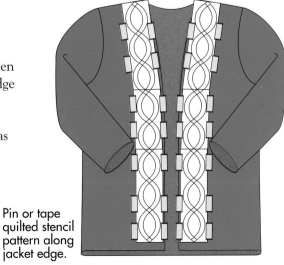

Pin or tape quilted stencil pattern along jacket edge.

Diagram A

Quilting the Jacket Border (*continued*)

3. Alternate the thread and bobbin thread colors so that the thread matches the reverse side. Check the tension so that the stitching appears balanced on both sides.

4. Stitch the border pattern, using 12 to 15 stitches per inch. The shorter stitch length makes it easier to stitch evenly around the curves (**Diagram B**).

5. Gently remove the stencils by tearing away the paper after all the stitching is complete (**Diagram C**).

6. To insert detachable shoulder pads:

• Apply a temporary adhesive, such as Res•Q Tape to the top edge of the shoulder pads (**Diagram D**).

• Position the shoulder pads in place (**Diagram E**). When you want to wear the opposite side of the jacket as the right side, remove the shoulder pads and reposition them on the reverse side.

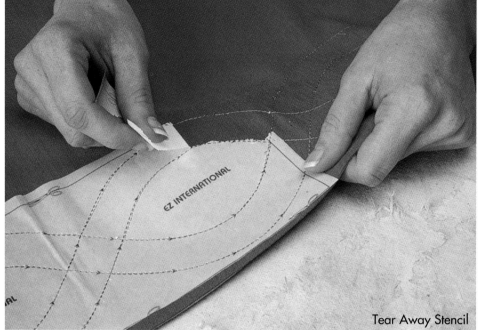

Tear Away Stencil

Stitch-Thru Tear Away Stencils

Pin the paper stencils to the fabric, stitch through the stencils, and then tear away the heavy-duty glazed paper.

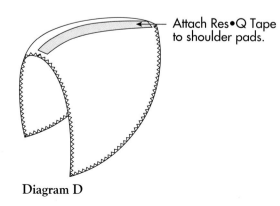

Stitch border pattern.

Diagram B

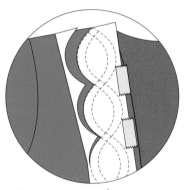

Tear away stencils.

Diagram C

Res•Q Tape

Res•Q Tape is a double-sided clear adhesive tape that instantly tacks the shoulder pads to the jacket. It can be easily removed when you wish to reverse your jacket.

Attach Res•Q Tape to shoulder pads.

Diagram D

Insert shoulder pad.

Diagram E

Reversible Top

A reversible top can give you a choice of color and style options. You can achieve two looks in about the same amount of time it takes to sew one top!

Reversible print top

Reversible pink top

Sewing the Inner and Outer Tops

1. Trim the hem allowances on the pattern to ⅝" **(Diagram A)**.

2. To stitch the necklines and the armholes:

• With right sides together, pin the inner front section to the outer front section, matching the armhole and neck edges. Stitch the armhole and neck edges. Grade the seam allowances **(Diagram B)**.

• Press the seam allowances flat and then open. Turn right side out and press.

• With right sides together, pin the inner back section to the outer back section, matching the armhole and neck edges. Stitch the armhole and neck edges. Grade the seam allowances.

• Press the seam allowances flat and then open. Do not turn right side out.

3. To join the inner and outer tops at the shoulder seams:

• Slip the front sections between the back sections, matching the shoulder edges and the seams.

• Stitch the shoulder seams in a circle and grade the seam allowances **(Diagram C)**.

4. To sew the underarm seam:

• With right sides together, pin underarm seams. Each underarm seam is double the normal length, since both the inner and outer seams are sewn at one time.

• Stitch the side seams, leaving an 8" opening in one side seam (see page 90).

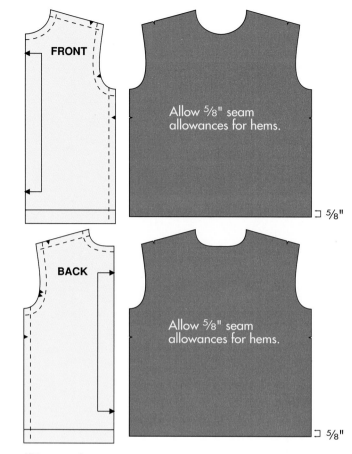

FRONT

Allow ⅝" seam allowances for hems.

⌐ ⅝"

BACK

Allow ⅝" seam allowances for hems.

⌐ ⅝"

Diagram A

Note from Nancy: *Each shoulder seam will form a circle. Since two tops are sewn at once, the sewing process is slightly different!*

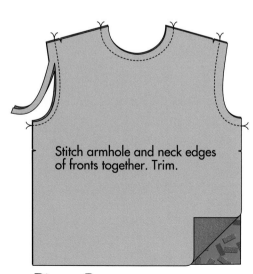

Stitch armhole and neck edges of fronts together. Trim.

Diagram B

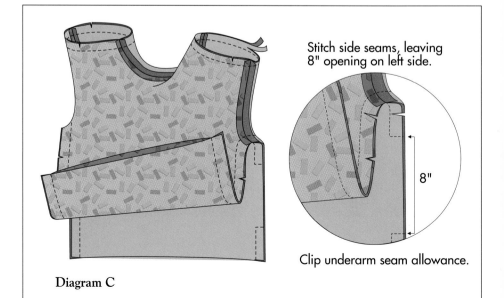

Stitch side seams, leaving 8" opening on left side.

8"

Clip underarm seam allowance.

Diagram C

• Press the seam allowances flat and then open.

• Clip the underarm seam allowance so that it lies flat.

• Turn the top right side out by pulling the shoulder seams to the outside through the lower edge.

• Press the neck and armhole seams. Slip the top over the end of the ironing board and check to see if the lower edges are even. Trim any uneven areas.

5. To hem the lower edge:

• Turn under ⅝" on the lower edge of the inner and outer top at one side seam. Pin the turned under edges together, matching seams (**Diagram D**).

Note from Nancy: Pinning the side seams together at the hems gives you a point of reference when you pull the hems to the outside through the side seam opening.

• Pull the pinned edges to the outside through the opening.

• Remove the side seam pins and repin the entire lower edge, with right sides together and seams matching.

• Stitch the lower edges together. Grade the seam allowances and press the seams flat using a seam roll (see page 92).

• Turn the top right side out through the opening (**Diagram E**).

• Handstitch the side seam opening closed (**Diagram F**).

6. To finish the outer edges:

• Turn the outer top to the outside.

• Roll the finished edges between your fingers to center the seam; press.

• With matching or monofilament thread, edgestitch the finished neck, armholes, and lower edges, always starting and stopping at a seam (**Diagram G**).

Turn under ⅝" hem at side seams.

Diagram D

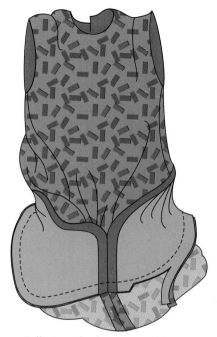

Pull pinned edges to outside.

Diagram E

Handstitch opening closed.

Diagram F

Edgestitch.

Diagram G

Express-ive Serged Reversibles

For those of you who are serger owners, using a decorative serger stitch along the outer edges is the ultimate in express-style reversibles. The sewing and serging are extremely streamlined since the wrong sides of the garments meet and the edges are simply joined with an overlock stitch. The only difficult decision is choosing which beautiful threads to showcase on your reversible!

Serged reversible jacket

Setting up the Serger

• Use a decorative thread in the upper and lower loopers, and a monofilament thread (see page 92, Wonder Thread) or a coordinating thread in the left needle.

• Adjust the stitch length to a slightly longer balance 3-thread overlock. Test on a scrap of fabric.

Reversible Serged Jacket

1. To construct the jacket:

• Sew the inner and outer jackets following the steps beginning on page 89. The only exception: don't leave an 8" opening in the inner jacket side seam. Press the seams flat and then open.

• Trim the shoulder seams of one jacket.

• With *wrong* sides together and raw edges aligned, pin the inner jacket to the outer jacket, matching notches and seams at the neckline, the sleeve hems, and the hemlines.

> **Note from Nancy:** *Round the corners by tracing the corner of a saucer or other small circle at each hemline of the center front. This simple rounding step will give you a continuous serger-express seam, eliminating the need to stop and start at the center front hemline.*

• Machine-baste at the ⅝" seam line around the neck, the front, the lower edge, and the sleeve openings. If the center front hem edge is at a right angle, round corners for easier serging **(Diagram A)**.

> **Note from Nancy:** *When serging in a circle, it is important to keep the exposed edge tidy and straight. The serging starting gate technique will help you start on the right track. Cut a 2" section of the ⅝" seam allowance near a seam where you plan to start and end the stitching. Align the cut edges in the starting gate next to the serger blades.*

Machine-baste jackets together at front and sleeve openings.

Diagram A

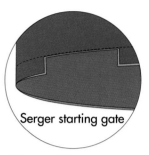

Serger starting gate

Diagram B

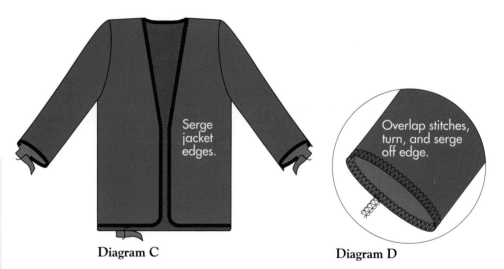

Serge jacket edges.

Diagram C

Overlap stitches, turn, and serge off edge.

Diagram D

2. To serge the jacket:

• Cut three serger "starting gates," one at the left side seam of the jacket and one at each underarm seam of the sleeve hems **(Diagram B)**.

• Serge the neckline, the center front, and the lower edges of the jacket. Guide the blade along the machine-basting stitches and trim the ⅝" seam allowance **(Diagram C)**.

• Upon reaching the starting gate, serge two stitches over the beginning stitches, guiding the fabric away from the blades or disengaging the upper blade to avoid cutting the previously serged stitches.

• Raise the presser foot, turn the fabric 90°, and lower the presser foot. Serge a 4" thread tail and cut the threads **(Diagram D)**.

(Continued on page 100)

Reversible Serged Jacket (*continued*)

3. Weave the thread tails into the serger stitches using a large- or double-eyed needle or a narrow loop turner. Lock the thread tail by applying a drop of Fray Check. Allow the Fray Check to dry before trimming off the thread tail.

4. To finish the jacket:

• With *wrong* sides together, pin the inner jacket to the outer jacket at the underarm and shoulder seams.

• Stitch in-the-ditch by hand in the underarm seams, 1" from the side seams, to keep the sleeves in place **(Diagram E)**.

• Handstitch in-the-ditch along the shoulder seam to attach the two jackets.

•Insert detachable shoulder pads (see page 94).

Reversible Serged Top

1. To construct the top:

• Sew the shoulder and underarm seams of each top, creating two separate tops. Press the seams flat and then open. Trim the shoulder seam allowances of the inner top.

• Turn the outer top right side out.

• With wrong sides together, pin the outer top to the inner top at the neckline, the armholes, and the hemline.

• Machine-baste at the ⅝" seam line around the neck, armhole, and lower edge openings **(Diagram A)**.

2. To serge the top:

• Cut four starting gates, one at the left side of the neck, one at the lower edge, and one at each underarm seam.

• Serge the neck, armhole, and lower edges of the top **(Diagram B)**.

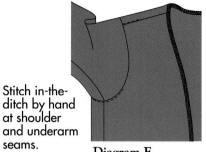

Stitch in-the-ditch by hand at shoulder and underarm seams.

Diagram E

Large-Eyed or Double-Eyed Needle

*You can weave thread tails into the serger stitches quickly with a **large- or double-eyed needle**. Thread the serger tail through the needle, insert the needle under the serger stitches for 1" to 2", and pull the tail through.*

Double-eyed needle

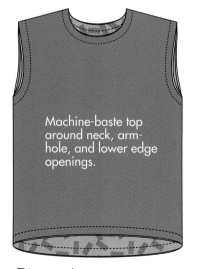

Machine-baste top around neck, armhole, and lower edge openings.

Diagram A

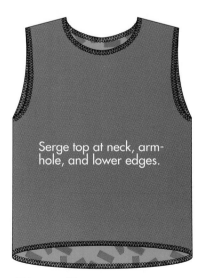

Serge top at neck, armhole, and lower edges.

Diagram B

Reversible Skirt

Lightweight fabric is the key to a bulk-free, versatile, reversible skirt. You will be amazed at the ease and speed with which you can sew this garment!

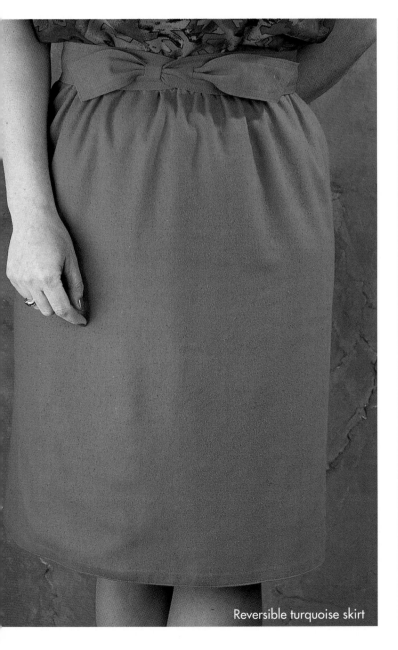

Reversible turquoise skirt

Reversible hot pink skirt

Sewing the Inner and Outer Skirts

1. To trim the hem and waist allowances on the pattern:

• Trim the waist casing to 1¾" (above waist mark).

• Trim the hem allowances to ⅝" **(Diagram A)**.

2. To create two separate skirts:

• Stitch the side seams of the outer skirt **(Diagram B)**. Press the seams flat and then open. Turn right side out.

• On the inner skirt, leave a 1" opening in one side seam, ¾" below the raw edge at the waistline **(Diagram C)**. This opening will be used to insert the elastic in the casing. Reinforce the stitches above and below the opening. Press the seams flat and then open.

3. To join the inner and outer skirts:

• Insert the outer skirt inside the inner skirt, with right sides together.

• Pin the lower edges of the inner and outer skirts together, matching the raw edges, the centers, and the seams.

• Stitch. Press the seam allowances flat and then open using a Seam Stick or seam roll **(Diagram D)**.

• Turn the outer skirt to the right side.

4. Roll the finished hem edge between your fingers to center the seams, pin, and edgestitch (see page 92) **(Diagram E)**.

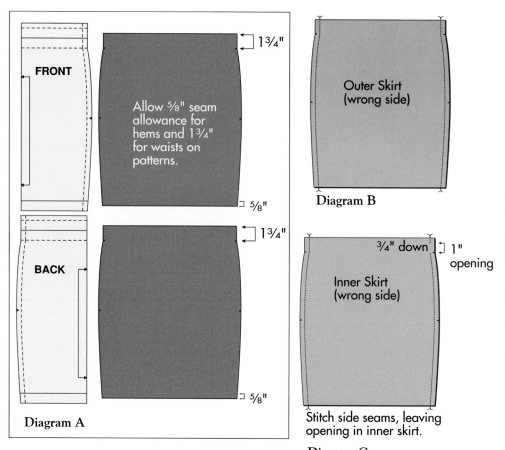

FRONT

1¾"

Allow ⅝" seam allowance for hems and 1¾" for waists on patterns.

⅝"

BACK

1¾"

⅝"

Diagram A

Outer Skirt (wrong side)

Diagram B

¾" down 1" opening

Inner Skirt (wrong side)

Stitch side seams, leaving opening in inner skirt.

Diagram C

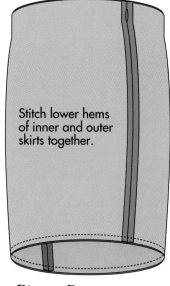

Stitch lower hems of inner and outer skirts together.

Diagram D

Edgestitch.

Diagram E

5. To prepare the upper edge for the casing and the elastic:

• Trim each side seam allowance within the casing area. Place a narrow strip of Stitch Witchery, Pellon's Wonder-Under, or a length of Thread-Fuse under the seam allowances, cover with a press cloth, and fuse with a steam iron (**Diagram F**).

Note from Nancy: To prevent frustration when trying to insert the elastic, I fuse or sometimes baste seam allowances to the garment in the casing area. If the seam allowances are left "free," it's easy to get the elastic caught underneath the seam allowance. Use this tip with all casings for express-style sewing!

• Slip the skirt on the end of the ironing board and check to see if the upper edges are even. Trim any uneven areas.

• Turn under ⅝" on the upper edge of the inner and outer skirts. Pin the turned-under edges together with folded edges even (**Diagram G**).

• Edgestitch close to the folds.

• Stitch again, 1" from the first stitching on the upper edge, to form the casing (**Diagram H**).

6. To prepare the elastic:

• Cut ¾"-wide elastic to a comfortable waist measurement.

• Cut a 2" square of fabric. Securely stitch or zigzag one end of the elastic to the center of the remnant square (**Diagram I**).

Note from Nancy: I like to use a square scrap of sturdy, light-colored fabric to anchor the elastic ends to form a circle. This eliminates the bulk created when the two elastic ends are overlapped.

(Continued on page 104)

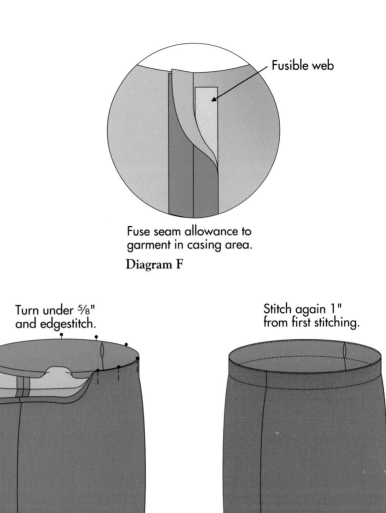

Fusible web

Fuse seam allowance to garment in casing area.

Diagram F

Turn under ⅝" and edgestitch.

Stitch again 1" from first stitching.

Diagram G

Diagram H

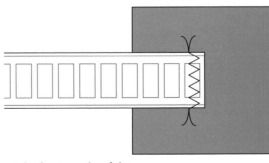

Stitch elastic end to fabric square.

Diagram I

Sewing the Skirts (*continued*)

7. To finish the casing:

• Insert the elastic through the casing, using a safety pin or an Ezy-Pull Bodkin.

• Place the remaining elastic end on the square. Butt the ends and securely stitch or zigzag in place **(Diagram J)**. Cut away the excess fabric scrap close to the long edges of the elastic.

• Tuck the elastic into the casing. Handstitch the opening in the casing closed **(Diagram K)**.

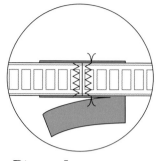

Diagram J

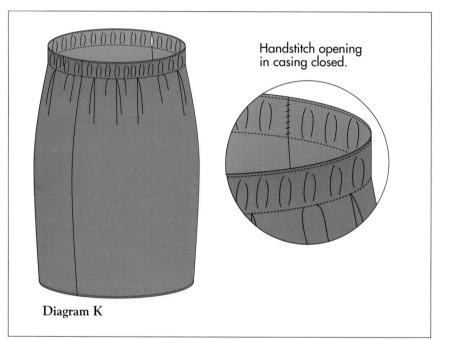

Handstitch opening
in casing closed.

Diagram K

Ezy-Pull Bodkin
*I prefer using the **Ezy-Pull Bodkin** for inserting elastic into a casing. The special "teeth" grip the elastic so that it doesn't get lost inside the casing. And the narrow tool is easy to navigate through the casing.*

Ezy-Pull Bodkin

Reversible City Shorts

Shorts are no longer just for play. Wear them for casual events with a simple top or add a jacket for a more professional look. Either way shorts are one of today's wardrobe classics. And reversible shorts make this basic even more adaptable. Like the other reversibles, the sewing sequence is unique, giving professional results!

Reversible hot pink city shorts

Reversible print city shorts

Sewing the Inner and Outer Shorts

1. Trim the hem allowances on the pattern to ⅝" and the waist to 1¼" (**Diagram A**).

2. To stitch the outer shorts:

• With right sides together, match the shorts front and back at the side seams and inside leg edges; stitch (**Diagram B**). Press the seam flat and then open. Repeat for second leg. Turn one leg right side out.

• With right sides together, insert one leg inside the other, matching edges of the crotch seam; stitch (**Diagram C**).

• Restitch inside the curve of the seam to reinforce the crotch area. Trim the seam allowances close to the second stitching line.

• Press the seam allowances open above the notches.

• Turn right side out.

> **Note from Nancy:** *The techniques on finger-pinning, Chapter 3 page 76, could easily be applied to sewing the side seams in shorts. Check out other chapters for hints that could apply.*

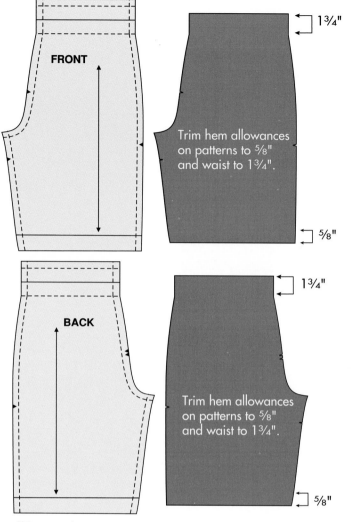

FRONT

Trim hem allowances on patterns to ⅝" and waist to 1¾".

1¾"

⅝"

BACK

Trim hem allowances on patterns to ⅝" and waist to 1¾".

1¾"

⅝"

Diagram A

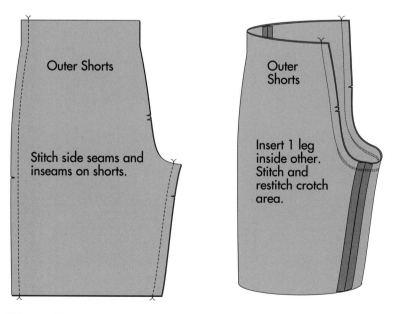

Outer Shorts

Stitch side seams and inseams on shorts.

Outer Shorts

Insert 1 leg inside other. Stitch and restitch crotch area.

Diagram B

Diagram C

3. To stitch the inner shorts:

• Stitch the inner shorts sections the same as the outer shorts, but leave a 1" opening in one side seam ¾" from the raw edge at the waist. This will form the opening for the elastic casing **(Diagram D)**.

• Press the seams flat and then open.

4. To join the inner and outer shorts:

• With wrong sides together, slip the inner shorts into the outer shorts, matching seams.

• Turn under ⅝" on the lower edge of the inner and outer shorts at the seams. Pin inner and outer shorts together at the seams **(Diagram E)**.

5. To hem shorts:

• Insert your hand through the waist edge between the inner and outer shorts. Pull the pinned edges to the outside.

• Repin the lower leg edge, with right sides together and seams matching; stitch.

• Grade the seam allowances and press the seams flat **(Diagram F)**.

• Insert the seamed edge back through the waist opening.

• Repeat for the second leg.

6. Center the hem seams and edgestitch, following the steps for the Reversible Jacket on page 92 **(Diagram G)**.

7. Prepare the upper edge of the shorts for the casing and the elastic. Insert the elastic following the steps for the Reversible Skirt, beginning on page 103.

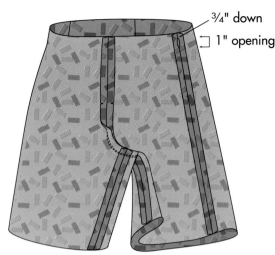

¾" down
☐ 1" opening

Stitch inner shorts, leaving 1" opening in side seam.

Diagram D

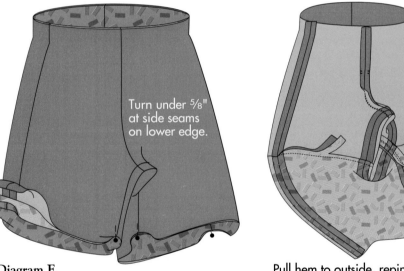

Turn under ⅝" at side seams on lower edge.

Diagram E

Pull hem to outside, repin hem, and stitch.

Diagram F

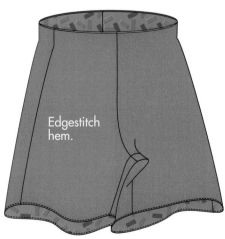

Edgestitch hem.

Diagram G

Accessories

Add creative accents and a personal touch to your wardrobe with these fashion accessories. Almost all pattern pieces are rectangles and require a minimum of fabric. Speedy sewing and serging tips throughout help you "sew up" projects in no time at all. Best of all, many of the accessories can be created for gifts!

Scarves for Accents

Scarves can add a simple or dramatic accent to your outfits. The dazzling Rosette Scarf and the Pouf Wrap Scarf can be stitched with express techniques and worn with style.

Rosette Scarf

Rosette Scarf

I found a scarf, with a sky-high price tag, similar to this design in a trendy boutique. You can create this Rosette Scarf, with a nominal investment in fabric and time, and achieve the same high-ticket look.

Fabric and supplies:
- ¼ yard of silk or silk-like fabric
- One nylon snap

To make the scarf:

1. Cut a 9" x 38" rectangle from the fabric.

2. To stitch the scarf edges:
- For machine stitching:
— Turn the edges under ¼" and stitch close to the fold.
— Turn under again and stitch, encasing the raw hem.
- Or serge the scarf edges:
— Round each corner by tracing the shape of a saucer to achieve a gradual curve. Trim the excess fabric.
— Set the serger for a rolled edge, using a lightweight thread that matches the fabric in the needle and the looper.

> **Note from Nancy:** *I always check my serger stitch on a scrap of fabric prior to actually sewing projects. In this case, test the stitch length to make certain that the stitches aren't too close together, which could cause the rolled edge to literally pull away from the lightweight fabric.*

— Serge the edges, making certain that the stitch is set at a medium length.

3. Draw a 10" line 3½" from one lengthwise edge. Repeat at the other end of the scarf.

4. To gather each end:
- Backstitch to secure the thread and then sew a basting stitch along each side of the 10" line. Stitch from the center to the edge of the scarf. Repeat at the other end of the scarf (**Diagram A**).

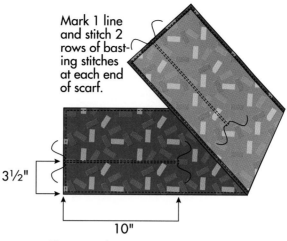

Mark 1 line and stitch 2 rows of basting stitches at each end of scarf.

3½"

10"

Diagram A

Stitch through center of gathers.

Diagram B

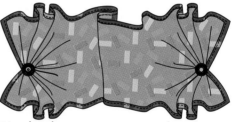

Handstitch snap sections to each end.

Diagram C

- Pull the bobbin threads tightly to gather the fabric at each end. Thread the loose bobbin threads through a hand-sewing needle and secure the gathers.

5. On the right side of the fabric, stitch through the center of the gathers to permanently hold them in place (**Diagram B**).

6. On the wrong side of the fabric, handstitch a snap section at each end over the center of the gathers (**Diagram C**).

7. Slip the scarf around your neck and snap closed. For an additional accent, attach a decorative button on the right side of the scarf over the snap.

Pouf Wrap Scarf

The Pouf Wrap Scarf is a favorite at my office. It can be stitched in less than 30 minutes. The gathers at one end gracefully drape on your shoulders or around your neck, and the scarf always retains its shape.

Fabric and supplies:
- ¼ yard of silk or silk-like fabric
- One Velcro dot

To make the scarf:
1. Cut a 9" x 31" rectangle from the fabric.

2. To form the rounded scarf end:

- Fold the fabric in half lengthwise, with raw edges aligned; press.

- Unfold the fabric. From one short end, draw a 9" line along the center crease.

- Backstitch to secure the thread and then sew a basting stitch along each side of the 9" line **(Diagram A)**.

- Refold along the basting stitches, with right sides together and raw edges aligned. Stitch the short end with a ¼" seam. Press the seam open **(Diagram B)**.

Pouf Wrap Scarf

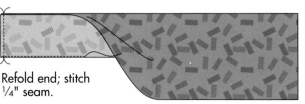

Baste along each side of 9" line.

9"

Diagram A

Refold end; stitch ¼" seam.

Diagram B

112

3. To finish the scarf edges:

• Leave the straight end unfinished.

• Turn under ¼" on the remaining edges and stitch close to the fold. Trim close to the stitching (**Diagram C**).

• Turn under again and stitch, encasing the ¼" raw hem.

4. To gather the rounded end:

• Pull up the bobbin thread tightly to gather the fabric.

• Thread the loose bobbin thread through a hand-sewing needle and secure the gathers (**Diagram D**).

5. To make a tuck at the opposite short end:

• Fold the fabric in half lengthwise, right sides together.

• Draw a 3" stitching line 2" from the fold.

• Stitch along the marked line, securing threads at both ends (**Diagram E**).

• Press the tuck, bringing the seam to the center. Machine-baste the tuck in place (**Diagram F**).

• Fold the sides over the tuck. Zigzag the ends together (**Diagram G**).

6. To attach the Velcro dot:

• On the outside, stitch the hook half of the Velcro dot to the pleated end of the scarf, centering it over the seam.

• On the inside, stitch the loop half of the Velcro dot to the gathered end of the scarf, centering it over the gathers (**Diagram H**).

7. Wrap the scarf around your neck and secure with the Velcro dot.

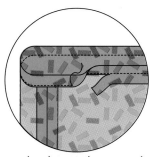

Finish edges with narrow hem, except for straight short end.

Diagram C

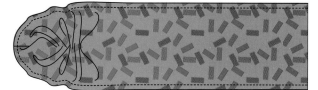

Gather end.

Diagram D

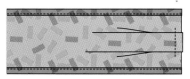

Mark 3" line and stitch.

Diagram E

2"

3"

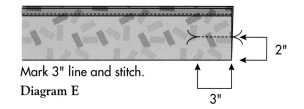

Center seam and baste short end.

Diagram F

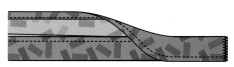

Fold under free edges and zigzag ends.

Diagram G

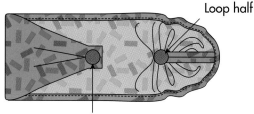

Loop half

Hook half

Attach Velcro dot.

Diagram H

Detachables

For an express-ive and express change, button on a detachable to a favorite blouse or shirt. The first detachable creates graceful folds and cascades down the front of the blouse. The next three detachables are sewn with the ultimate fabric for streamlined sewing—Ultrasuede! These accessories only take a few inches of fabric—¼ yard or less—so the investment is nominal, but the look is dynamic!

Detachable Cascade

Detachable Cascade

Stitch your favorite print or use coordinating fabrics to make cascading detachables that match different outfits.

Fabric and supplies:
- ⅜ yard of lightweight fabric
- 4" length of ⅛" elastic
- 2 small buttons

To make the cascade:

1. Cut a 10" x 40" crosswise rectangle from the fabric.

2. To stitch the vertical seam:

• Fold the fabric in half lengthwise, right sides together and raw edges aligned. Stitch using a 1½" seam, leaving a 4" opening near one end for turning **(Diagram A)**.

• Press the seam flat and then open, using a Seam Stick (see page 41) to prevent the edges from leaving an imprint.

• Center the seam and stitch the lower edge. The extra-wide seam allowance acts as interfacing after the tube is turned.

3. Trace the blouse neckline on the unstitched end of the tube. Add a ¼" seam allowance and cut out **(Diagram B)**.

4. Cut two 2" lengths of ⅛" elastic. Fold each piece in half to form a small loop. Insert the loops into the tube near the sides and align the cut edges. Stitch the neckline seam, catching the edges of the elastic **(Diagram C)**.

5. Trim and clip the seam. Turn right side out through the opening and press. Handstitch the opening closed.

6. Measure 8" from the top of the strip and mark the first buttonhole in the center of the tube. Measure and mark two more buttonholes 8" apart. Stitch the buttonholes **(Diagram D)**.

7. To attach the cascade to your blouse:

• Stitch small buttons to the blouse neckline under the collar to match the loops of the cascade. Fasten the elastic loops over the buttons to secure.

• Button the second blouse button through the first cascade buttonhole. Continue to button.

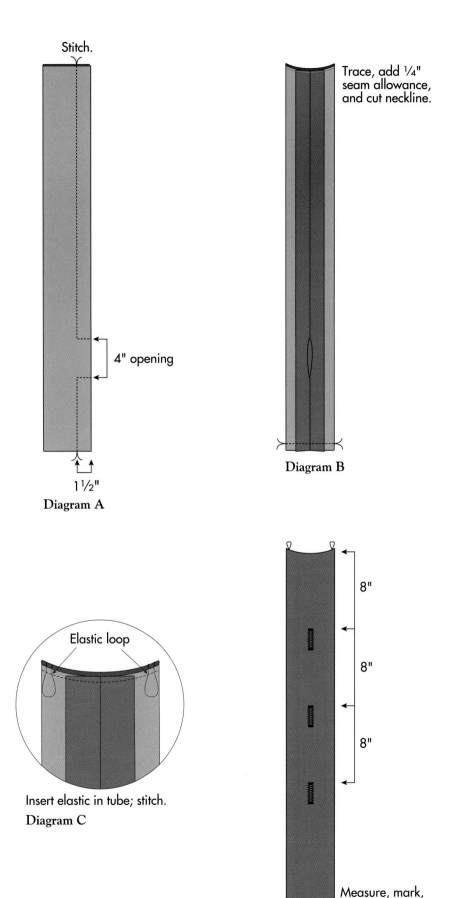

Stitch.

4" opening

1½"

Diagram A

Trace, add ¼" seam allowance, and cut neckline.

Diagram B

Elastic loop

Insert elastic in tube; stitch.
Diagram C

8"

8"

8"

8"

Measure, mark, and stitch buttonholes.

Diagram D

No-Sew Ultrasuede Detachable

This geometric design has great style and flair. You can transform a small piece of Ultrasuede into a contemporary accessory with a few quick cuts.

Fabric and supplies:
• 2" x 22" (or as long as your blouse) rectangle of Ultrasuede
• Iron-on stabilizer
• Buttonhole Cutter Set or X-acto knife

To make the detachable:
1. Cut a 2" x 22" rectangle of iron-on stabilizer for the pattern.

2. Align the center of the iron-on stabilizer at the center front of the blouse, matching the top of the strip to the neckline stitching line. Mark buttonholes to correspond to those on the blouse.

3. Remove the stablizer from the blouse. Mark 1" x 2" rectangles between buttonhole markings on the stabilizer. Draw geometric designs within those rectangles using the full-size patterns shown on page 141 or your own design.

No-Sew Ultrasuede Detachable

Totally Stable

*Machine embroidery enthusiasts iron **Totally Stable** onto the wrong side of the fabric before embellishing with thread and tear away the stabilizer after sewing. It works equally well for this cutwork-style detachable.*

***Totally Stable** temporarily sticks to the fabric when pressed in place, preventing the design from shifting. If you do not have iron-on stabilizer, household freezer paper will adhere to fabric in the same way. However, you'll need to hold the design and freezer paper up to a window to trace the design, since freezer paper is opaque.*

Totally Stable

4. To cut out the design:

• Press the iron-on stabilizer pattern to the wrong side of the fabric with a dry iron.

• Place the strip, pattern side up, on a rotary cutting mat. Use an X-acto knife or a Buttonhole Cutter Set to cut the buttonhole slits and the cutwork design. Cut through the iron-on stabilizer and fabric **(Diagram)**.

5. Peel away the iron-on stabilizer.

6. Button the No-Sew Ultrasuede Detachable to the blouse through the buttonholes. Now, that's express style!

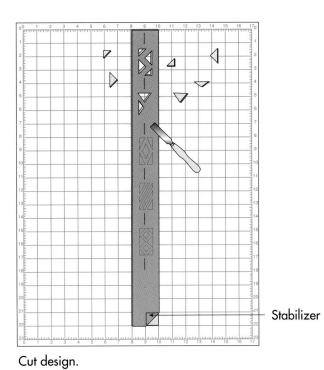

Stabilizer

Cut design.

Diagram

Buttonhole Cutter Set

*It is easy to make neat, professional-looking button-holes or geometric designs in Ultrasuede with the **Button-hole Cutter Set**. Simply place the section to be cut over the block and cut with the cutter. If the design line is smaller than the cutter, place half of the line over the edge of the block and cut. Repeat the steps for the second half of the line.*

Buttonhole Cutter Set

Woven Ultrasuede Detachable

You can make a striking detachable quickly by weaving two strips of Ultrasuede with narrow strips of different colors.

Fabrics and supplies:
- Three colors of Ultrasuede:
  — Back strip: one color
  — Front strip: one contrasting color
  — Weaving strip: one complementary color
- 1¼"-wide strip of fusible interfacing

To make the detachable:

1. Cut the following Ultrasuede strips:
- Cut one back strip to measure 2" x 22" or the length of the blouse.
- Cut one front strip of the contrasting Ultrasuede to measure 1½" x 22" or the length of the blouse.
- Cut three strips to measure ¼" x 22" (or slightly longer than the back strip), cutting two from the backing color and one from the complementary color.

2. Mark and cut vertical buttonholes on the backing strip to correspond to those on the blouse.

Woven Ultrasuede Detachable

3. To cut crosswise slits on the top strip:

• Measure ½" from the top of the strip and cut a ¾" horizontal slit, centering the slit on the strip **(Diagram A)**.

• Measure ½" from the first slit, center, and cut another ¾" horizontal slit.

• Measure 2" from the second slit and cut a ¾" horizontal slit.

• Continue for the entire length of the front strip.

4. Weave the ¼" strips through the slits in the front strip.

• Start with a ¼" strip of backing fabric. Using the Ezy-Pull Bodkin (see page 104), weave the strip over each ½" slit, positioning it at the far left of the slit **(Diagram B)**.

• Weave the complementary color strip under each ½" strip. Butt the strip next to the first strip **(Diagram C)**.

• Weave the final strip of the backing color over each ½" strip. Position it at the far right of the slit **(Diagram D)**.

5. Cut a 1¼" strip of fusible interfacing slightly shorter than the length of the top strip. Fuse it to the back of the top strip to keep the woven strips in place **(Diagram E)**.

6. Center the wrong side of the front strip on the right side of the backing strip. Edgestitch in place, securing the strip at the sides, the top, and the bottom with a size 70 denim/sharp needle or a Microtex/sharp needle **(Diagram F)**.

7. Trim any weaving strips that extend beyond the backing and front strips. Button on through the back slits—and enjoy!

Needles for Ultrasuede

A denim/sharp needle or the new Microtex/sharp needle pierces the dense microfibers of Ultrasuede and makes seaming a breeze. These needles are available in a wide range of sizes, but the size 70 needle works best on Ultrasuede.

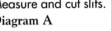

Measure and cut slits.
Diagram A

Weave strip #1.
Diagram B

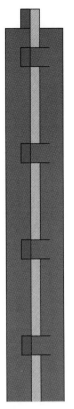

Weave strip #2.
Diagram C

Weave strip #3.
Diagram D

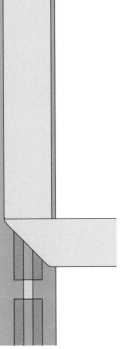

Fuse interfacing to back.
Diagram E

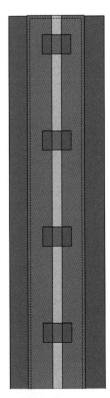

Add backing strip; edgestitch.
Diagram F

Appliqué Detachable

Here's another express-ive, quick change for your blouse. Use Ultrasuede scraps to make this great-looking detachable. It's simple to make, yet it adds a new dimension to a basic garment.

Fabrics and supplies:
- 9" x 12" rectangle of Ultrasuede for the top and the back
- 9" x 6" piece of contrasting Ultrasuede for the appliqué
- Wonder-Under
- Stitch -N-Tear
- Wash-Away Stabilizer

To make the detachable:

1. Cut two layers (one for the back and one for the front appliqué) of Ultrasuede the same size as the full-size pattern shown on page 141. Also cut one each of the four triangles in the full-size pattern.

2. Mark and cut the top buttonhole on the center of the backing layer. Cut the remaining buttonholes corresponding to the buttonholes on the blouse **(Diagram A)**.

3. To apply the appliqué pieces with Wonder-Under:
- Trace the geometric shapes (see page 141) to the paper side of the Wonder-Under **(Diagram B)**.
- Place the rough side of the Wonder-Under against the wrong side of the Ultrasuede scraps.
- Using a hot, dry iron, fuse the Wonder-Under to the wrong side of the appliqué fabrics for three seconds. Let the fabric cool.
- Cut out the shapes and peel away the paper backing **(Diagram C)**.
- Place the appliqués, fusible side down, on the top layer of the detachable as shown on the pattern.
- Cover the appliqué pieces with a damp press cloth and fuse **(Diagram D)**.

Appliqué Detachable

Mark and cut buttonholes.

Diagram A

Trace shapes on paper side of Wonder-Under.

Diagram B

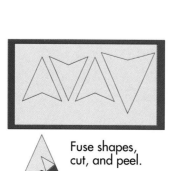

Fuse shapes, cut, and peel.

Diagram C

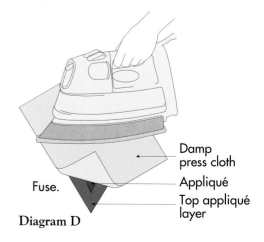

Damp press cloth

Appliqué

Top appliqué layer

Fuse.

Diagram D

4. Back the fabric with a temporary stabilizer such as Stitch-N-Tear. Straightstitch around the edges using monofilament thread (see Wonder Thread, page 36) in the needle or satin-stitch the edges using machine embroidery thread or metallic thread (**Diagram E**). Remove the temporary stabilizer.

5. On the wrong side of the backing layer, apply a thin line of fabric glue, such as Liqui Fuse, along the edges. Place the wrong side of the appliqué layer over the right side of the backing layer, matching edges.

6. Sandwich all the layers between two pieces of a temporary see-through stabilizer, such as Wash-Away Stabilizer, and edgestitch or satin-stitch the layers together (**Diagram F**). Remove the stabilizer.

7. Trim any Ultrasuede backing that extends beyond the edges of the appliqué.

8. Button the detachable to your blouse.

Back with temporary stabilizer and stitch around appliqué edges.

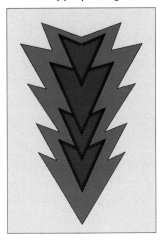

Diagram E

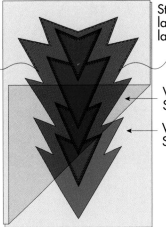

Stitch appliqué layer and back layer together.

Wash-Away Stabilizer

Wash-Away Stabilizer

Diagram F

Liqui Fuse

*Liqui Fuse is a liquid fusible web that is perfect to use on hard-to-pin fabrics like Ultra-suede. Apply a thin line of the glue-like fusible to the wrong side of the fabric and set permanently by pressing. **Liqui Fuse** is washable and dry cleanable and can be removed if the garment is washed before the Liqui Fuse is pressed.*

Liqui Fuse

Wash-Away Stabilizer

This water-soluble stabilizer makes edgestitching a breeze on appliqués. The stabilizer gives your sewing machine foot and the feed dogs better control when stitching edges together. After stitching, gently tear away the larger sections of the stabilizer. Any stabilizer remaining around the stitches washes away with water in seconds.

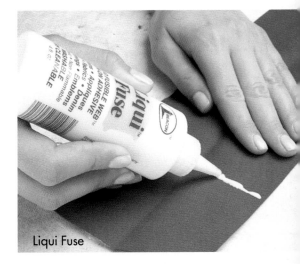

Wash-Away Stabilizer

Express Belts

Finding just the right belt to accent an outfit can be time-consuming and sometimes frustrating. Here's an alternative—make a collection of belts! You can be the designer and creator, and the one-of-a-kind results can be exactly what you're looking for.

Reversible Ultra Slit Belt

Reversible Ultra Slit Belt

Reversible Ultra Slit Belt

You can make this reversible belt in 20 minutes with only ⅛ to ¼ yard of Ultrasuede. Many stores sell Ultrasuede by the inch, making this an affordable option! You'll love how easy it is to work with this soft, luxurious fabric that is available in a wide variety of brilliant, luscious colors. Since Ultrasuede is a nonwoven fabric, it does not ravel, which makes seaming a breeze.

Fabric and supplies:
- Two 2"-wide strips of Ultrasuede in two colors (four strips for waist measurements greater than 31")
- Liquid adhesive or silk pins

To make the slit belt:
1. Cut the following strips from Ultrasuede:
- For a waist measurement up to 31", cut a strip the waist measurement plus 14". Cut another strip the same size from the second color **(Diagram A)**.
- For a waist measurement greater than 31", cut two strips by the waist measurement plus 14". Cut two more strips from the second color.
  — Overlap the short ends ½".
  — Use a fabric glue stick or a liquid adhesive, such as Liqui Fuse (see page 121), or silk pins to temporarily hold the two layers together.
  — Join the strips together with two rows of topstitching. Stitch ⅛" from the cut edge. Stitch a second row ¼" from the first row of stitching.
  — Cut the belt to the correct size (waist measurement plus 14"), placing the seam at the center back. Repeat with second color of strips.

(Continued on page 124)

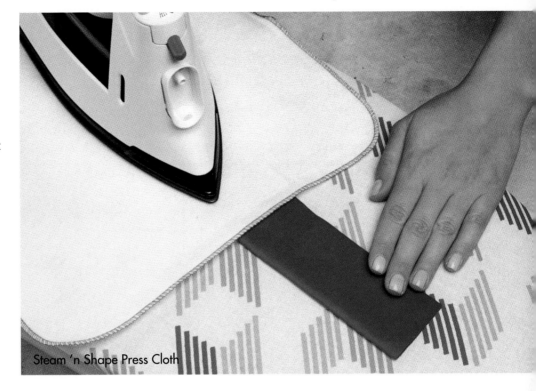

Steam 'n Shape Press Cloth

Note from Nancy: *Ultrasuede is an extremely dense fabric, which makes it difficult to pin. The finer the pin, the easier it will pass through the fabric. I use silk pins for any Ultrasuede pinning.*

Steam 'n Shape Press Cloth
This cloth is ideal to use when pressing Ultrasuede. The extra-absorbent press cloth enables the iron to produce the steam Ultrasuede requires, while protecting the right side of the fabric from the heat of the iron.

Diagram A

Waist measurement + 14"

2"

Reversible Ultra Slit Belt (*continued*)

2. Place the wrong sides of the two strips together and cut the edges even. Pin or use Liqui Fuse (see page 121) to temporarily hold the layers together.

3. To taper the belt ends:

• Measure and mark 1" from one belt end along one edge. Draw a diagonal line with chalk from the mark to the corner. Cut along the line (**Diagram B**).

• Repeat for the other end.

4. Edgestitch around the belt, stitching ⅛" from the edge and using a size 70 denim/sharp or Microtex/sharp needle (see page 119). Add a second row of stitching ¼" from the edge (**Diagram C**).

5. To mark the positions for the belt slits:

• Fold the belt in half, short ends together and edges aligned. Mark the center back.

• Fold a tape measure, bringing the finished end of the tape to the number marking your waist measurement.

• Place the fold of the tape measure at the center back fold of the belt. The finished end of the tape measure indicates the position for the belt's center front. Mark the center front positions on each end of the belt (**Diagram D**).

6. To cut the slits:

• Cut a vertical ⅝" slit in the center of the belt at one of the center front markings using a Buttonhole Cutter Set (see page 117).

• Cut two ⅝" slits each ½" from the opposite center front marking (**Diagram E**).

• Edgestitch around the slit openings.

7. To wear the belt:

• Working from the right side of the belt, weave one end of the belt through the double-slit opening.

• Bring the opposite belt end from the underside through the single slit (**Diagram F**).

• Adjust the belt ends so that the belt fits snugly around the waist.

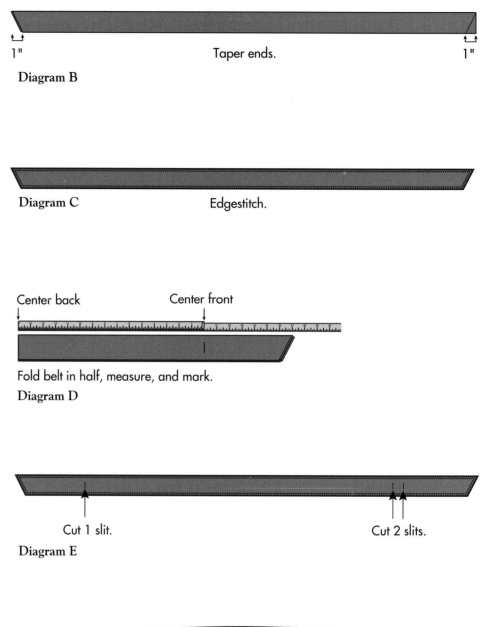

1"   Taper ends.   1"

Diagram B

Diagram C   Edgestitch.

Center back   Center front

Fold belt in half, measure, and mark.
Diagram D

Cut 1 slit.   Cut 2 slits.
Diagram E

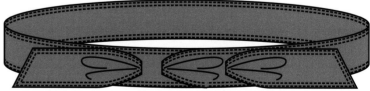

Diagram F   Weave ends through slits.

Express-ive Appliqué Belt

Here's a belt that's sure to be a hit, either in your own wardrobe or as a gift. This express belt includes an appliqué on the front and a Velcro closure on the back.

Fabrics and supplies:
- ¼ yard of Ultrasuede
- Contrasting scraps of Ultrasuede
- Scraps of Wonder-Under
- 1½" strip of 2"-wide Velcro tape

To make the appliqué belt:
1. To make the belt pattern piece:
- Cut a paper strip 3½" wide by your waist measurement plus 3". To locate the center front, fold the paper in half with the short ends together.
- Measure 9" from the center fold and mark both edges **(Diagram A)**.
- At the unfolded end, measure ¾" down from the top edge and ¾" up from the bottom edge and mark.
- Draw a line from the 9" mark, tapering to the top ¾" mark. Repeat on the bottom edge. Cut out the pattern.

2. Cut two belt pieces from the Ultrasuede.

3. To add the appliqués to the belt front:
- Draw your own designs or use the full-size designs on page 140.
- Fuse the appliqués to the belt front using Wonder-Under and stitch around the appliqués **(Diagram B)**.

4. With wrong sides facing, place the belt front and the belt back together. Edgestitch ⅛" from all the outer edges **(Diagram C)**.

5. To attach the Velcro closure:
- Position the Velcro loop section on the outside of the belt on the right short end, ½" from the edge.
- Position the hook section on the inside of the belt on the left short end, ½" from the edge. Trim the Velcro to fit the shape of the belt.
- Stitch around each strip.

6. To wear, secure with the Velcro closure at the center back.

Express-ive Appliqué Belt

3½" Taper ends to 2" at cut edge. **¾"** **2"** **¾"**

9"

Diagram A

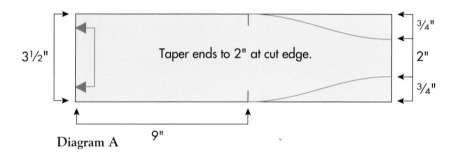

Fuse appliqués to belt front.

Diagram B

Place belt front to belt back; edgestitch.

Diagram C

Express-Style Totables

Totes come in handy for anyone on the go. Make these totes from vinyl-coated or quilted fabric, canvas, denim, Ultrasuede, or any other medium- to heavyweight woven fabric.

Trio of Totes

Use the large tote for clothes or shoes, the medium size for hair spray and shampoo, and the small size for a quick change of jewelry. Keep in mind that a trio of these totes makes an excellent gift!

Fabric and supplies:
• ½ yard of 45"-wide fabric (Yields one large, one medium, and two small totables or one large and two medium totables.)
• Zippers: 7" for the small, 14" for the medium, and 22" for the large totables.

To make a tote:
1. Cut a fabric rectangle the size needed for the desired tote:
• Small: 6" x 12" rectangle
• Medium: 12" x 18" rectangle
• Large: 18" x 24" rectangle
2. Fold the fabric with the short ends together and mark the center of one long edge with a short nip.
3. To create handles for the totable:
• Cut fabric pieces the size needed:
— Small: 2" x 6" strip
— Medium or large: 2" x 8" strip
• Zigzag or overlock the long edges. Fold the edges to the center, wrong sides together.

Totables

Position handle; baste.

Diagram A

• Zigzag or stitch with a double needle down the center of each strip on the right side of the handle.
• Fold the completed handle in half, with the short ends together.
• Position the folded handle over the nip with the looped end toward the middle of the tote; baste **(Diagram A)**.

Note from Nancy: *If you are making several totables, cut a long 2"-wide strip of fabric, stitch down the center, and cut it into 8" sections. Or, for the fastest technique, cut 6" to 8" lengths of grosgrain or satin ribbon to use as handles.*

4. To insert the zipper:

• With right sides together, align one of the short ends of the fabric with the right zipper tape edge. Align the bottom zipper stop with the bottom cut edge of the fabric. Stitch a ¼" seam **(Diagram B)**.

Note from Nancy: Each zipper is purposely longer than the opening of the tote. The extra length makes it possible to avoid sewing next to the zipper pull, which often causes a crooked seam.

• Repeat, meeting the left zipper tape edge with the remaining short fabric edge, right sides together. Stitch **(Diagram C)**.

5. From the right side, edgestitch next to the fold of the fabric on each side of the zipper **(Diagram D)**.

6. To stitch the top seam:

• Pull the zipper tab down. This is very important! The partially open zipper enables you to turn the tote right side out after stitching the lower seam.

• With wrong sides together, fold the fabric rectangle, centering the zipper and the handle ends. Make certain the zipper tab is *below* the seam line. Stitch or serge the top seam with a ¼" seam allowance. Restitch the seam in the center to reinforce the zipper area **(Diagram E)**.

7. To stitch the lower seam:

• Refold the tote so that the center of the zipper is aligned along one side edge.

• Stitch or serge the bottom seam. Restitch in the zipper area to reinforce the seam **(Diagram F)**.

• Trim the excess zipper tape.

• Turn the tote right side out.

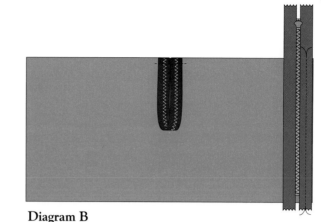

Stitch zipper to 1 short end.

Diagram B

Stitch zipper to other short end.

Diagram C

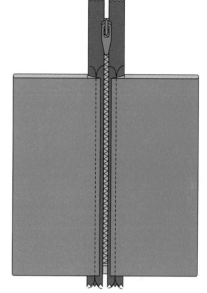

Edgestitch next to fold.

Diagram D

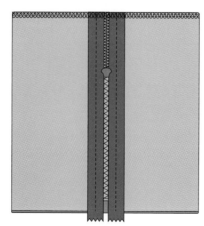

Center zipper; stitch end with zipper top stop.

Diagram E

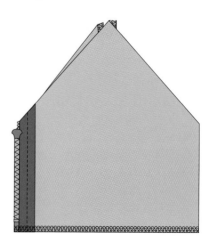

Refold tote; stitch end with zipper bottom stop.

Diagram F

127

Zip-Up Cosmetic Bags

Here are two cosmetic bags that are a perfect fit for most handbags or overnight cases. Like the totes, the sewing is express-style!

Fabric and supplies:

- ½ yard of reversible quilted fabric (Yields one small and one large cosmetic bag.)
- Two 14" zippers (one each for small and large bag)

To make a cosmetic bag:

1. Cut the following pieces for the cosmetic bags (**Diagram A**):

- Small:
  — Front/Back: 9" x 12" rectangle
  — Upper front: 2" x 9" strip
  — Loop: 2" x 5" strip
- Large:
  — Front/Back: 12" x 15" rectangle
  — Upper front: 3" x 12" strip
  — Loop: 2" x 5" strip

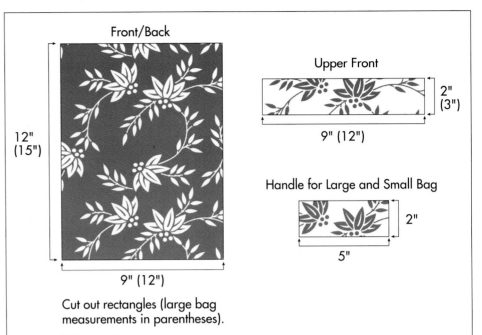

Front/Back

12" (15")

9" (12")

Upper Front

2" (3")

9" (12")

Handle for Large and Small Bag

2"

5"

Cut out rectangles (large bag measurements in parentheses).

Diagram A

Cosmetic bags

2. Clean-finish all the raw edges.

3. To insert the zipper:

• Fold under ⅝" on one lengthwise edge of the upper front section and press.

• Fold under ⅝" on one short edge of the front/back section and press **(Diagram B)**.

• Position the folded edge of the upper front section along the right zipper teeth, with the zipper facing up and the tab extending above the edge. Stitch the fold to the zipper.

• Position the folded edge of the front/back section along the left zipper teeth. Align the edges of the two sections. Stitch **(Diagram C)**.

• Open the zipper and bar-tack across the teeth at the top opening, close to the edge. Trim the excess zipper tape above the bar tack. Close the zipper.

4. Create the bag handle, using the same techniques detailed for the totes, pages 126 and 127.

5. To position the handle on the bag:

• Fold the handle in half.

• With the loop toward the center, align the handle ends with the left edge of the upper front section, just above the zipper top. Pin **(Diagram D)**.

6. To shape the bag bottom:

• Fold the fabric in half, right sides together and edges aligned; pin.

• Measure and mark 1" (1½" for the large bag) from the lower fold along each side seam.

• Turn up the lower fold to the 1" mark (1½" mark for the large bag) **(Diagram E)**. Pin.

7. To finish the bag:

• Stitch or serge the top with a ¼" seam, making sure the handle is not caught in the seam.

• Open the zipper halfway, providing an opening to turn the bag right side out.

• Wrap the top seam toward the bottom, folding the seam at the stitching line (see page 38). Stitch the side seams from the wrapped corner to the lower fold with a ¼" seam **(Diagram F)**.

• Trim the seams and turn right side out.

Upper Front

Front/Back

Fold under ⅝" on lengthwise edge of upper front and short edge of front/back.

Diagram B

Stitch folded edges to zipper.

Diagram C

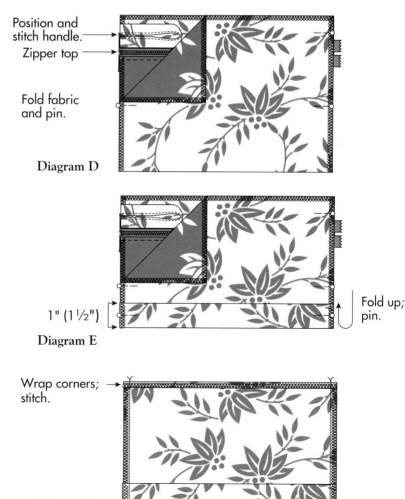

Position and stitch handle.

Zipper top

Fold fabric and pin.

Diagram D

1" (1½")

Fold up; pin.

Diagram E

Wrap corners; stitch.

Diagram F

Zip-Up Handbag—Express-ive Option

Create an elegant handbag in 60 minutes or less, using the same express-style sewing sequence used to sew the cosmetic bags. Try stitching specialty fabrics such as Ultrasuede, brocade, Ultraleather, leather, or suede to create different looks from one design.

Fabrics and supplies:
- ⅜ yard of fabric (NOTE: If you use Ultrasuede, you can make three hand-bags from ⅜ yard of fabric.)
- 12" zipper
- ¼ yard of lining fabric (if not using Ultrasuede)

To make the handbag:

1. Cut the following pieces for the handbag:
- Front/Back: 9" x 17" rectangle
- Upper front: 2½" x 9" strip
- Strap: Cut 1½"-wide strips of Ultrasuede, Ultraleather, or leather, piecing as needed to equal 54". Or use a 54" length of chaining or cording.
- For the appliqué shapes, cut from leather or suede scraps.

2. To make the handbag shapes, follow the directions for creating the cosmetic bags (pages 128 and 129) with these modifications:
- Apply appliqués with Wonder-Under to one end of the bag front. Refer to the appliqué instructions on pages 120 and 121 (Appliqué Detachable). See page 140 for patterns for appliqué shapes.

3. To assemble the bag:
- If lining the handbag, cut lining pieces the same size as the handbag rectangles.
- Place the fashion fabric and the lining rectangles with wrong sides together and raw edges aligned. Machine-baste around the outer edges and treat the two layers of fabric as one.
- To create the suede/leather strap, fold the 1½" strip in half lengthwise, wrong sides together. Edgestitch. Align

Zip-Up Handbag

Position and stitch strap to handbag.

Diagram

the raw edges of the strap with the top edge of the handbag. Stitch in place **(Diagram)**.

4. To finish the bag, follow steps 6 and 7 on page 129 for the Zip-Up Cosmetic Bags.

Curl 'n' Go Curling Iron Caddy

The sewing is fast on this curling iron caddy but, best of all, the inner Teflon-coated lining allows a hot curling iron to be packed without fear of scorching the caddy fabric!

Fabrics and supplies:

• ⅓ yard each of reversible 45"-wide quilted fabric, Teflon-coated fabric, and Wonder-Under

• ⅓ yard of matching fabric for bias binding

To make the caddy:

1. Cut the following:

• Reversible quilted fabric: one 9" x 14" rectangle for the caddy and one 4½" x 9" rectangle for the pocket.

• Teflon-coated fabric: 9" x 14" rectangle

• Wonder-Under: 9" x 14" rectangle

• Matching fabric: cut 2"-wide bias strips, piecing as needed to equal 45".

2. To fuse the Teflon-coated fabric and quilted fabric together:

• Place the fusible side of the Wonder-Under to the wrong side of the Teflon-coated fabric and fuse. Remove the paper backing.

• Place the Wonder-Under side of the Teflon-coated fabric to the wrong side of the quilted fabric and pin. Cover the holder with a damp press cloth and fuse (Diagram A).

3. To shape the caddy:

• Trace the shape of a cup or a saucer at the lower corners of the rectangles with a marking pen.

• Cut through all the layers along the marked lines (Diagram B).

(Continued on page 132)

Curling iron caddy

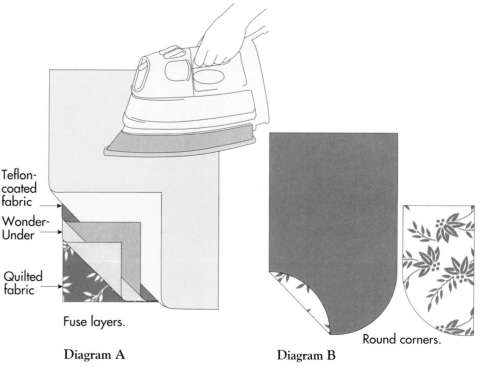

Teflon-coated fabric

Wonder-Under

Quilted fabric

Fuse layers.

Diagram A

Diagram B

Round corners.

Curling Iron Caddy (*continued*)

4. To add bias binding to the pocket and the holder:

• Cut 2"-wide bias strips, using a rotary cutter, a quilting ruler, and a cutting mat.

• Join the strips by sewing the short ends together with ¼" seam allowances. Continue piecing as needed to equal 45". Press the seams open and then flat. Trim seams to align with the edges of the strips (**Diagram C**).

• Fold the joined bias strip in half lengthwise, with wrong sides together and raw edges aligned. Press lightly to make a crease. Open the strip. Fold the raw edges toward the center crease and press. Or use a Bias Tape Maker for express bias tape.

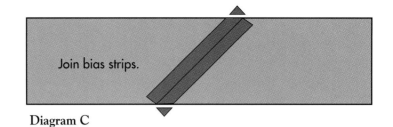

Join bias strips.

Diagram C

Rotary Cutter, Quilting Ruler, and Cutting Mat

For express sewing, use this cutting trio to quickly and accurately cut bias strips. The rotary cutter's sharp blade easily and accurately cuts one or more layers of fabric while the transparent ruler makes it effortless to measure the strip width.

Rotary cutter, quilting ruler, and cutting mat

Bias Tape Maker

*The **Bias Tape Maker**, an express notion, quickly and neatly folds under the raw edges of bias strips. Slip the bias strip wrong side up through the wide end of the tape maker and slide the fabric through the funnel-shaped tube. Press the folded tape at the narrow end. The lengthwise edges will automatically fold to the center. The size of the **Bias Tape Maker** indicates the width of the strip after the raw edges are pressed to the center. The 1" size is best suited for garment construction.*

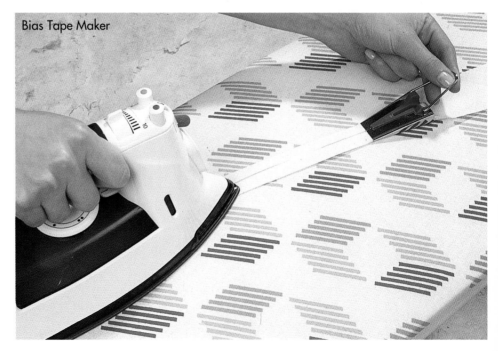

Bias Tape Maker

• Stitch the bias tape to the upper edge of the caddy and the caddy pocket (**Diagram D**).

• Clean-finish the straight vertical edge of the pocket with an overlock or zigzag stitch (**Diagram E**).

5. To add the pocket to the holder:

• Place the pocket, reverse side down, on the holder along the bottom left side. Align the edges and pin.

• Stitch ⅜" from the long, straight edge through all layers (**Diagram F**).

• Press the pocket back over the seam allowance. Machine-baste the raw edges together (**Diagram G**).

6. Fold the caddy in half lengthwise, with Teflon-coated sides together. Machine-baste the raw edges together (**Diagram H**).

7. To stitch the bias tape to the outer edges of the caddy:

• With a steam iron, lightly press the bias tape to preshape the tape to match the curves of the caddy.

• Unfold the bias tape and turn under a ¼" hem along one short end and finger-press.

• With right sides together, align the long raw edge of the bias tape with the raw edge of the caddy. Place the short folded end of the tape at the lower edge (**Diagram I**). Pin.

• Extend the bias tape 5" beyond the top of the caddy to allow for a short handle. Stitch, following the fold line of the tape.

• Wrap the bias tape over the edge, covering the stitching with the remaining folded edge. Edgestitch the bias tape in place, stitching through all layers (**Diagram J**).

• Turn under the raw edge of the handle, lapping the end ½" over the upper edge of the holder. Stitch in place (**Diagram K**).

Stitch bias tape to upper edge of caddy and upper edge of pocket.

Diagram D

Clean-finish long, straight edge.

Diagram E

Stitch pocket to caddy.

Diagram F

Press pocket over seam allowance; baste.

Diagram G

Fold caddy in half; baste.

Diagram H

Stitch bias tape to raw edge; extend tape 5" at top.

Diagram I

Diagram J

Stitch end to holder.

Diagram K

Jewelry Hang-Up

Keep your jewelry safe when you travel with this combination padded hanger and jewelry organizer. The see-through zippered compartments can be folded up and concealed inside the hanger cover.

Fabrics and supplies:

- ⅔ yard of 45"-wide reversible quilted fabric
- 13" x 15" rectangle of clear vinyl
- ⅓ yard of matching or contrasting fabric for bias strips
- Three 14" zippers
- 15" strip of ¾"-wide Velcro tape
- Optional: scraps of Ultrasuede for appliqué
- One hanger
- Two sheets of 8½" x 11" lined paper

Clear Vinyl

Clear vinyl is a terrific "fabric" to use when sewing travel accessories. In the finished project, you can see everything that you have stored. But vinyl's sticky surface can make it difficult to feed through your machine's feed dogs and presser foot. The solution? Place ruled paper under the vinyl. The paper allows the vinyl to feed easily under the presser foot, while the lines give a straight sewing guide.

Jewelry Hang-Up

Jewelry Hang-Up

To make the jewelry hang-up:

1. Cut one 13" x 15" pocket section and two 10" x 18" hanger cover sections from quilted fabric.

2. To create a hanger cover:

• Stack the two 12" x 18" quilted pieces, with right sides together and raw edges aligned.

• Place the hanger on top and trace the sides. Trace ½" outside the first line for seam allowances and extend the sides an additional 5". Cut out the cover **(Diagram A)**.

3. To create the hanger opening and hem the lower edges:

• Locate the center opening for the hanger by folding each section in half, short edges together.

• Measure and mark 1½" on each side of the center. Make a nip at each mark. Press under ¼" between the nips and edgestitch **(Diagram B)**.

• Press under a ½" hem along the lower edge of each section.

• Position the Velcro hook tape over the hem of the back section and stitch in place along both edges. Position the loop tape over the hem of the front section and stitch.

4. To stitch the zippers to the vinyl:

• Matching lines, tape the sheets of paper together to make a rectangle slightly larger than the vinyl piece.

• Position the vinyl on the paper so that the upper edges are even.

• Using the lines as a guide, position the first zipper horizontally on the vinyl, 1" from the top of the 15" edge and ½" from the left edge **(Diagram C)**.

• Attach a zipper foot and set the stitch length for 10 to 12 stitches per inch. Edgestitch the zipper to the vinyl/paper along both edges.

(Continued on page 136)

5"

½" Trace hanger; add seam allowances.

Diagram A

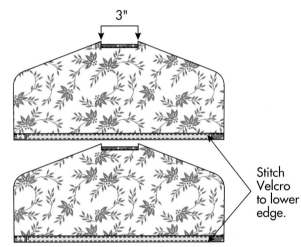

3"

Stitch Velcro to lower edge.

Edgestitch top opening and lower hem.

Diagram B

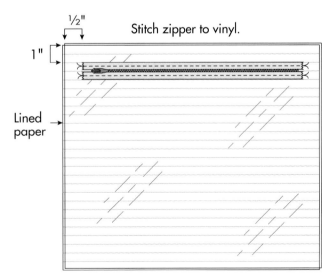

½"

Stitch zipper to vinyl.

1"

Lined paper

Diagram C

Jewelry Hang-Up (*continued*)

• Position the second zipper 4" and the third zipper 7" from the top edge of the vinyl; stitch (**Diagram E**).

• Turn the vinyl over and gently tear away the paper.

• With appliqué or embroidery scissors, carefully cut away the vinyl from the back of the zipper teeth, leaving a narrow seam allowance (**Diagram F**).

5. To create the pockets:

• Position the vinyl on the right side of the quilted fabric. Restitch along the top row of stitching of the second and third zippers to make the pockets (**Diagram G**).

• Divide the zipper area into thirds and use the edge of Sewer's Fix-it Tape (see page 69) as a stitching guide.

• Stitch the compartments from the bottom of each pocket to ¼" from the zipper teeth but do not stitch through the zipper teeth (**Diagram H**). Remove the paper.

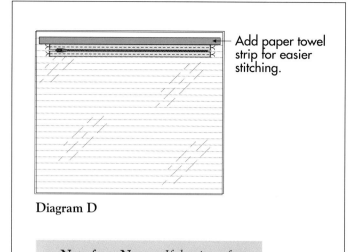

Add paper towel strip for easier stitching.

Diagram D

Note from Nancy: If the zipper foot gets stuck on the vinyl, place a strip of paper or a paper towel on the vinyl next to the zipper tape. This will make it much easier to sew (**Diagram D**).

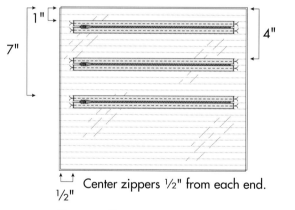

1"

7"

4"

½"

Center zippers ½" from each end.

Diagram E

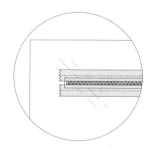

Remove paper and trim vinyl away from zipper.

Diagram F

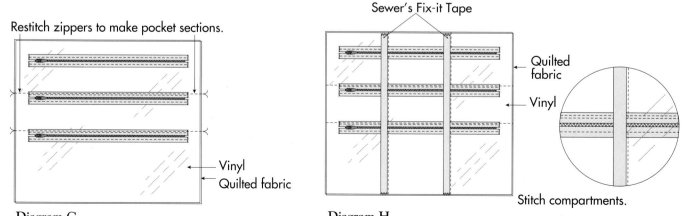

Restitch zippers to make pocket sections.

Vinyl
Quilted fabric

Diagram G

Sewer's Fix-it Tape

Quilted fabric

Vinyl

Stitch compartments.

Diagram H

6. To finish the pocket section:

• Trace around a cup or a saucer to round off the lower corners and cut.

• Bind the edges with bias tape (see bias tape instructions on page 132) **(Diagram I)**.

7. To join the pocket section to the hanger cover:

• With the wrong side up, measure and mark 1½" up from the lower edge of the back hanger and 1" from each corner.

• Align the upper corners of the pocket section with the marks.

• To stitch the layers together, edgestitch along both edges of the bias binding strip **(Diagram J)**.

• With right sides together and raw edges aligned, stitch or serge the side seams of the hanger sections together **(Diagram K)**.

• Turn right side out and insert the hanger.

• Fold the pocket section into thirds and conceal inside the hanger cover. Close the lower edge with the Velcro tape **(Diagram L)**.

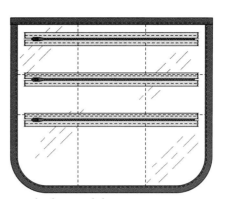

Bind edges with bias tape.

Diagram I

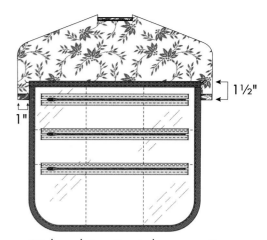

1½"

1"

Stitch pocket section to hanger section.

Diagram J

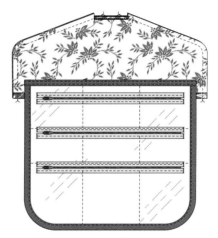

Stitch side seams of hanger sections.

Diagram K

Fold up pockets to conceal.

Diagram L

Organizer Tote

No matter where you're headed, chances are you need a carryall. The perfect carryall—an Organizer Tote. Select one of your favorite fabrics—denim, vinyl, quilted reversibles, or upholstery. Then, in about 60 minutes, create this tote with six (three front and three back) side pockets.

Fabric and supplies:
- 1½ yards of 45"-wide fabric
- 5" strip of ¾"-wide Velcro tape
- Optional: 4" x 15" piece of cardboard or plastic canvas

To make the tote:

1. Cut out the following for the tote bag **(Diagram A)**:
- Panel: 21" x 31" rectangle
- Strap: two 4½" x 49" strips
- Pockets: 21" x 23" rectangle

2. To complete the tote panel:
- Press under ¼" and then 1" on both 21" edges of the tote panel. Edgestitch along all the folds.
- Serge or finish the sides with a zigzag stitch.

3. To complete the six pockets:
- Press under ½" twice along both 21" edges of the pocket section. Edgestitch.
- Serge or finish the side seams with a zigzag stitch.
- With wrong sides together and 21" edges aligned, fold the tote panel in half. Mark the center of the panel. Repeat with the pocket section.
- Place the wrong side of the pocket section on the right side of the tote, matching center marks and edges. Pin. Machine-baste the panel sides to the tote **(Diagram B)**.
- Measure and mark 2½" from each side of the center. Stitch along these lines to form the pocket bottoms.
- To determine the strap placement, mark vertical lines on the right side of the fabric, 6" from each lengthwise edge.

Organizer Tote

Sewing Machine Needles

If stitching denim or canvas, use a size 100 denim/sharp sewing machine needle. You'll be surprised how the right needle size will streamline the sewing process.

Selvage

Straps
4½" x 49"

Tote panel
21" x 31"

Pockets
21" x 23"

Pattern layout

Diagram A

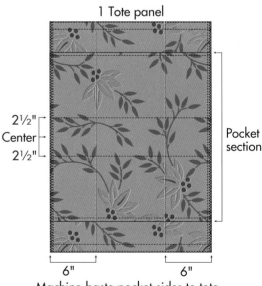

1 Tote panel

2½"
Center
2½"

Pocket section

6"   6"

Machine-baste pocket sides to tote.
Mark vertical lines for strap placement.
Stitch.

Diagram B

4. To complete the straps:

• With right sides together, align the short ends of each strip. Stitch using a ¼" seam to create a continuous strap. Press the seams open.

• With wrong sides together, fold the lengthwise edges to the center. Press (**Diagram C**).

> *Note from Nancy: I recommend using a press cloth when you press vinyl fabric. Direct contact with a hot iron will cause the vinyl to stick to the iron.*

• Fold the strap a second time, aligning the folded edges. The strap should measure approximately 1¼" wide. Press (**Diagram D**). Edgestitch along the fold.

> *Note from Nancy: If you are using quilted or non-vinyl fabric, keep the strap folds even by inserting stitch witchery in the fold and fusing in place.*

5. To attach the straps to the tote:

• Pin the strap along the vertical marks, centering the seams of the strap on the base of the tote. (Centering the seams will allow even lengths of handles.)

• Edgestitch the strap to the tote panel, stitching along both edges of the strap. Reinforce the stitching at the top of the tote (**Diagram E**).

6. Center the Velcro sections between the straps on the inside of the tote. Edgestitch in place (**Diagram F**).

7. Fold the tote, right sides together, and stitch the tote side seams, beginning at the top and continuing to the base. Press seams flat and then open (**Diagram G**).

8. To miter each lower corner:

• Fold the tote, wrong side out, so that a triangular point forms, aligning the side seam with the center of the base.

• Stitch across the lower edge of triangle from one pocket base to the next. Restitch for reinforcement (**Diagram H**).

• Trim and finish the seam, if desired.

• Turn the tote right side out.

Fold lengthwise edges to center. Press.

Diagram C

Fold again and press.

Diagram D

Velcro

Center Velcro between straps; stitch.

Velcro

Diagram F

Edgestitch strap to tote.

Diagram E

Stitch side seams.
Diagram G

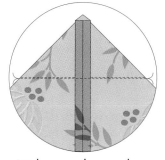

Stitch across lower edge of triangle. Restitch.

Diagram H

*P*atterns

Use these full-size patterns
to complete your projects.

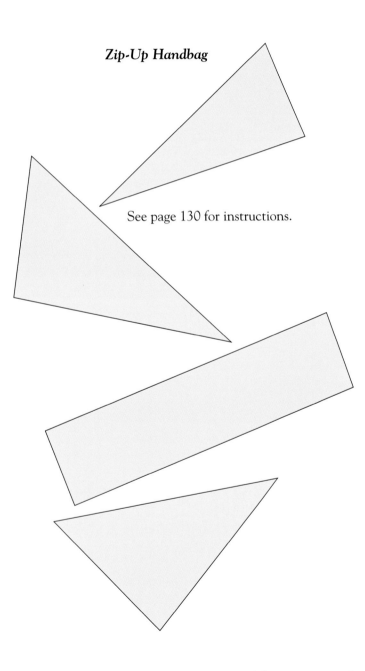

Zip-Up Handbag

See page 130 for instructions.

*Express-ive
Appliqué Belt*

See page 125 for instructions for
the Express-ive Appliqué Belt.

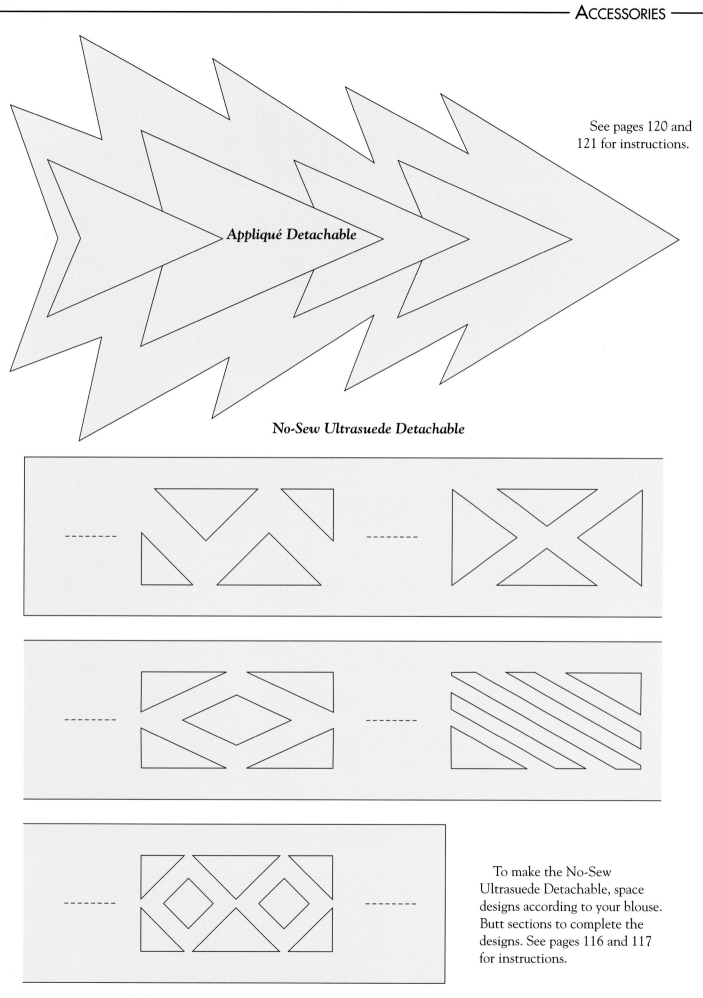

See pages 120 and 121 for instructions.

Appliqué Detachable

No-Sew Ultrasuede Detachable

To make the No-Sew Ultrasuede Detachable, space designs according to your blouse. Butt sections to complete the designs. See pages 116 and 117 for instructions.

INDEX

Nancy Zieman—businesswoman, home economist, and national sewing authority—is the producer and hostess of the popular show "Sewing With Nancy," which appears exclusively on public television stations. The show, broadcast since September 1982, is the longest-airing sewing program on television. Nancy organizes each show in a how-to format, concentrating on step-by-step instructions.

Nancy also produces and hosts *Sewing With Nancy* videos. Each video contains three segments from her television program. Currently, there are 28 one-hour videos available to retailers, educators, libraries, and sewing groups.

In addition, Nancy is founder and president of Nancy's Notions, which publishes *Nancy's Notions Sewing Catalog*. This large catalog contains more than 4,000 products, including sewing books, notions, videos, and fabrics.

Nancy has written several books including: *Let's Sew!, 10-20-30 Minutes to Sew,* and *The Best of Sewing With Nancy.* In each book, Nancy emphasizes efficient sewing techniques that produce professional results.

Nancy was named the 1988 Entrepreneurial Woman of the Year by the Wisconsin Women Entrepreneurs Association. In 1991, she also received the National 4-H Alumni Award. She is a member of the American Home Economics Association and the American Home Sewing & Craft Association.

Nancy lives in Beaver Dam, Wisconsin, with her husband/business partner, Rich, and their two sons, Ted and Tom.

For a complete line of sewing notions, turn to...

Nancy's Notions Sewing Catalog

• Nancy Zieman's catalog for sewing, serging, and quilting enthusiasts.
• More than 4,000 products, including books, notions, videos, fabrics, and supplies!
• Everyday discounts. Save up to 20%!
• 100% satisfaction guaranteed!

For your free *Nancy's Notions Sewing Catalog*, send your name and address to:

Nancy's Notions
P.O. Box 683
Dept. 2311
Beaver Dam, Wisconsin 53916

Or call 1-800-833-0690.